PEOPLES
AND
POLICIES

PEOPLES
AND
POLICIES

A World

Travelogue

by BRIGADIER GENERAL FRANK L. HOWLEY,
U.S.A (ret.)

HENRY REGNERY COMPANY • CHICAGO • 1959

Library of Congress Catalog Information

Howley, Frank L.   1903–   Peoples and
policies; a world travelogue. Chicago, H.
Regnery Co., 1959. 211 p. 21 cm. 1. U. S.—
For. rel.—1953–   2. World politics—1955–
I. Title. E835.H62   327.73   59–10303 ‡

Contents

Acknowledgments

The author acknowledges his obligations to more than 265 persons throughout the world who, by answering his questions, explaining their problems, and pointing out conditions in their countries, have contributed greatly to the acquisition of the basic facts and local color upon which this book is based.

Particular thanks are due Orrin Wightman of New York and Henry Regnery of Hinsdale, Illinois, who have given help and encouragement. A special note of thanks goes to the Foundation for Foreign Affairs for its invaluable assistance in the preparation of the book.

It is obvious to the author that all travelers and writers on foreign affairs, whatever their points of view, should recognize their obligations to America's foreign correspondents—men and women who, often at personal risk and sacrifice, keep the American people informed of important day-by-day developments abroad.

FRANK L. HOWLEY

PEOPLES
AND
POLICIES

PART ONE
The Traveler and His Goals

1

Who Says So?

This is a travelogue through American foreign policy. It takes you to foreign countries whose relationships with our own require our attention. It tells you of people and places abroad, of their problems, as I have found them on my many travels during the past several years. Travelers see and hear mainly what they are looking for. What I have been looking for from African Ghana to Asian Tainan, from Cairo to Tel Aviv, from Vienna to Algiers, from Berlin to Hong Kong—where the Iron and Bamboo curtains lift a bit above the ground—has been the answer to one big question: What are we, the people of the United States, to think of these foreign countries, and what, if anything, are we to do about them? In each place I visited, the answer was as different as the conditions and problems I encountered. I found no clear-cut answer to my question, only answers. The answers I did find add up to a still bigger question: What kind of foreign policy must guide the United States in the years ahead?

I did not attempt to find a general, all-encompassing, easy formula, nor did I arrive at a conclusion that can be presented in a few simple words. If you look for theories or slogans, this book will offer neither. I have investigated only realities, and I have searched only for the right steps that we must take in each and every case. Under close inspection, many theories and slogans turn out to be nothing but words. At best, they give us the illusion that we know more about things than we really do. What is worse, they often mislead us toward actions which we do not really want to take and which we should not take, since they do not lead to the goals for which we strive.

In many a case, we have lost our aims in the jungle of our own words, which have blinded us to realities. Unhappily, this country has been—and still is—a victim of words as often as it has profited from words. Our enemies, in turn, have been—and are now more than ever—employing words as deliberate, efficient weapons to obscure realities. With great skill, the Soviet conspiracy is using words, not to describe things as they are, not to promote man's understanding of himself and the world, nor to reveal divine or mundane truths and to inspire love and tolerance, but to stir man to hate, to confuse his image of duty and destiny, to hurry him toward his destruction. Based on Communist philosophy as it has evolved from Marx and Engels through Lenin and Stalin to Khrushchev and as it underlies Communism and whoever runs and rules it at the moment, this deliberate, destructive misuse of words is a dangerous Soviet weapon. I have seen its disastrous effects throughout the world, whether people fall for it or fight against it.

Most of the victories the Soviets have won over us in the past decade have been won by words. Their propaganda has stirred up unrest in countries they planned to conquer, and it has softened up our own will to resist the Soviet advance with our moral, military, economic, and political power. And often have we fallen prey to our own words, that is, we accepted words based on theorems, on wishful thinking, on the disregard for facts in favor of generalities and prejudices and misinformation. A long list of slogans have acquired great respectability and have come to influence public opinion and thereby our public policy; fine as they sound, you will discover that they have little meaning or connection with reality if you study the facts on the spot, as I found when I checked some slogans of our foreign policy with the realities of foreign lands.

American public opinion must have sensed these fallacies of words recently, for a widespread and still increasing distrust of words, slogans, and theories can be observed throughout the land.

If this is a healthy sign, it is not without dangers; if it shows the resistance of Americans toward ill-employed words, it could also lead them to lose interest in the facts that underlie them, and this we cannot afford. "Never overestimate the information of the people, never underestimate their intelligence," the late columnist Raymond Clapper used to say; the danger is that because of their high intelligence, Americans will pass over important information altogether since to them it seems distorted by theorizers and propagandists. Yet it is only on the basis of information that we can use our intelligence to choose the correct, necessary, required actions. This may well be a choice between defeat and victory, between destruction and survival.

But how can Americans eager to learn the facts find their way through the avalanche of conflicting information which is offered them, without pause, from all sides? If they watch television or turn on their radios, if they open a magazine, a newspaper, a book, if they listen to sermons and speeches and conversations, they are regaled with more information than they can possibly digest; worse yet, one "expert" often tends to contradict the other. How to find one's way through this jungle of words? How to come closer to the truth?

The best way perhaps, and certainly a first step, is to ask that good old American question: "Who says so?" We can evaluate information and opinion only if we scrutinize the man who offers it; more precisely, if we ask first whether he is willing to present the facts or whether he has an axe to grind; second, whether he is experienced in observing and reporting facts or whether he is untrained and unable to do so; third, whether his record shows that he and his word can be trusted.

True, an argument or an opinion must be judged on its own merits rather than by a personal dissection of its author when it comes to purely academic discourse, in which everyone pursues the same goals from the same assumptions. But in the fields of political information and action, an opinion is often worth only as much as the man who presents it. This is particularly true when words and arguments are deliberately employed to deceive the listeners. When the Communists speak of peace or freedom, for instance, they surely do not mean what those to whom they address their words are bound to understand by these words. But let us find that it is a Communist who speaks, or a fellow-traveler, or one of those innocent dupes who consistently echoes Communist views without knowing their Communist source, and we will instantly be on guard.

Before I begin my report, the reader is invited to pop the question: "Who says so?" Here is my answer:

At present, I am vice-president of New York University, the world's largest privately supported university. But I speak for myself, by the same right by which every other member of this great academic institution can express, challenge, or approve ideas according to his lights. I am a retired brigadier general of the United States Army; needless to say, I do not speak for any official establishment either. While I was in active service, my experience with American foreign politics began. When our army of liberation entered Europe, I was military governor of Cherbourg and then of Paris, where the Soviets were already fastening their tentacles about the local government and where their propaganda against America was going full blast. I continued into Berlin, where I remained for four and one-half years, first as deputy commandant, then as commandant of the U.S. sector of this great city. In daily and nightly contact with our French and British allies and also with the democratic Germans who stood on our side, it was my lot to resist the Soviet power, which, after calling itself our ally in words, slowly and unmistakably turned out to be our enemy. They challenged us to the blockade battle of Berlin. We won. It was a victory as glorious as any won on the battlefield. *Berlin Command,* my report on the greatest Western battle and victory of the Cold War, is still considered a classic text on the strategy and tactics of dealing with Communists.

In Berlin during those days, I saw the Soviets as our enemy, yet when I publicly called them by this name and suggested that we treat them accordingly, criticisms from friend and foe were hurled on me; they were bitter and deeply discouraging. While American policy evolved and changed, I did my best, along with other Americans, to make it work. Of necessity, it changed from outright appeasement in 1945 to co-existence, when in an unspoken mutual agreement both sides agreed: "You run your side of the world, and we'll run ours." Only after we discovered that the Soviets, much as they accepted and encouraged this policy in words, used it as a shield behind which they prepared to take over from us and then run our side of the world, too, only then did our policy switch to containment, that is, to an attempt to resist forcefully all further expansion into our—and neutral— spheres, which the Soviets would undertake by force. For a while, we proceeded, again in words, to proclaim a policy of liberation designed to encourage the captive Soviet nations to escape to freedom, by force if necessary, but from then and there, the policy swung back to whence it had started, and appeasement of the Soviets became the order of the day again.

Throughout these twists and turns, I maintained that appeasement was suicidal, that containment was not enough, that co-existence was a detour to surrender, and that liberation would not do if, when, and as long as it was claimed and promoted only in and by words. I expressed my views freely in books, to the press, and at lectures. Those who disagreed said at first that I was wrong, but as the facts piled up during the years and sub-stantiated my argument, making it rather obvious that I had been right in the first place, they said: "Even if he was not wrong, at any rate it was then not timely for him to say so." To be called prematurely right seems a badge of honor, though it comes too late.

Since I left Berlin, I have gone every year to a new part of the world where our foreign policy encountered a serious challenge, either instigated or exploited by the Soviets. My travels have taken me throughout Europe, Asia, Africa, and the Americas. As in Berlin, I wanted to study the situation on the spot and to hunt down the facts before I made a decision. These facts very often showed a marked contrast to the words I had heard and read at home. What I found first and foremost was that to arrive at a decision, one has to make up his mind about the different sides of a question and its different risks, hopes, and challenges. I hope that my report will enable the reader to see the many and different sides to each question and that it will also help him to make up his mind about the right answer.

2 *In Search of Foreign Policy*

America's future depends on its foreign policy. This country will remain the land of the free and the home of the brave, or it will go down in defeat and disgrace, depending, of course, on the manner in which we utilize our military, economic, diplomatic, and spiritual powers. If we do it the right way, we shall overcome the present, clear, and great danger to our survival.

Today we are living, as Secretary of State John Foster Dulles put it and as most everybody knows, in "perilous times." If this be a commonplace, it yet spells out quite clearly the situation we face. What makes our times so perilous is, of course, the very existence of Soviet Communist power. It threatens our rights to life, liberty, and the pursuit of happiness; it will keep endangering us as long as it exists. Its leaders, from Lenin to Khrushchev, have never left any doubt about this. More than forty years ago, Lenin proclaimed that the greatest task of his regime was to instigate and carry through the international revolution, until freedom, faith, and human dignity perish from this earth. His words are still Communist dogma; only yesterday Nikita Khrushchev, with a self-certain grin, assured the leaders of the free world that "we will bury you." More important still, the Communist leaders have shown by their foreign policy—and their domestic policy, which is closely related to it—that in this and only in this aim they mean what they preach and that they act accordingly. They are out to destroy our way of life, our independence, all our values, and, given the power, determination, and shrewdness of their leaders, we have no reason to doubt it.

As Lenin set forth, again in accordance with Communist policies up to this very day, the Communists must instigate, exploit and control unrest and dissent everywhere to arrive at their goal. And today, their chances seem better than ever before, which is a second reason why our times are "perilous." All over the world, backward peoples, and even socially advanced peoples, are going through the pangs of a rapid evolution. It is driven on, with hurricane velocity, by modern communications, which can bring a sheik of Arabia to Washington in twenty hours or present a live Paris fashion show to a crowd watching television screens in what was once the Gold Coast and is now the Republic of Ghana. In African and Asian countries, new leaders seem suddenly willing, and perhaps able, to change their whole cultures along the economic and political pattern of industrialization and independence, often in a struggle against "the white man" of the West. Their evolutions would pose serious problems even if the Communists did not work full blast to turn them into revolution. In other countries, the Communists have already gained a foothold and use it to spread their influence. Their dominions of terror already reach from Berlin to Peiping. Finally, there remain the countries which the Soviet Union considers its immediate opponents and whose opposition it tries to weaken, to confuse, and to mislead in many ways. The battlefield is world wide.

With the United States as the chief power to oppose the Soviets and with every Soviet gain anywhere in the world tantamount to a loss of our own strength, our foreign policy has become the center of our defense; as long as there is no shooting war, there will be some form of struggle whose strategy is called foreign policy. There is hardly a place in the world which does not concern us in one way or another and in which we are not forced, or at least tempted, to take some kind of active position. The sum total of all our relationships with and of our actions toward foreign countries makes up our foreign policy.

Today, out of problems that seem unsolvable, out of the trials and errors of the past, an American foreign policy is being born, yet it remains difficult, if not misleading, to name its essence or to sum up all its phases under one single label in one slogan. The reason is that our present-day foreign policy was not devised by scholars or blueprinted by a Machiavelli or even drawn up by governmental planners; no one theory, easy to spell out and to explain, underlies it. Like Topsy—and also like other phases of our present-day policies and of our prevailing order in general— it just grew.

America has been in search of a foreign policy for a long time, in fact, since 1776. Even before the United States Department of State, originally known as the Department of Foreign Affairs, was created on January 10, 1781, this country had its makers of foreign policy. As early as 1775, the Committee of Secret Correspondence, consisting of five members, looked after American interests abroad. After two years, it was expanded to the Committee of Foreign Affairs, with ten members. The main job of these early authorities was to get arms for the Republic. Today, an organization of their size and scope could hardly provide the weapons for a single regiment, even if it were directed by a new Benjamin Franklin, who used to woo French women with his charm and win French men with his power of reasoning; in fact, these were the main tools with which he shaped American foreign policy from day to day.

The over-all directives for our foreign policy, or rather the lack of them, have remained as characteristics of that policy from the days of the early Republic up to these days of totalitarian peril. Then, as now, the American people had no desire for the land of other nations; then, as now, they lacked a guiding and general principle to be promoted, if not enforced, abroad—unlike, for instance, the British, who tried to undo the power of their potential foe on the Continent by building up an equally strong power of their foe's foes. This was how they came to direct their foreign policy according to the doctrine of the balance of (other peoples') power. Nor have the American people been obsessed by a common emotion toward a foreign nation which would dominate their own foreign policy, in the way, say, of French foreign policy, driven by hatred of Germany since the war of 1870 and continuing up to the aftermath of the second world war. And our democratic Republic has never had its foreign policy shaped by dictatorial lust for power either. Happily free from ruling autocrats, America has also been free from their foreign-policy interests, so strikingly formulated by the Bey of Algiers at the end of the eighteenth century: "If I were to make peace with everyone," he said, "what should I do with my soldiers? Unable to live on their simple allowances, they would cut off my head for want of other prizes."

Without a domestic doctrine that would have made it imperative for America to interfere in foreign-power relations and balances, without hatred of a foreign people, and without dictatorial self-interests, American foreign policy could well afford to aim at this country's splendid isolation, as George Washington proclaimed and as was done for more than a century. At the time, all this country desired was to live in peace and to be let alone; except for defense against foreign invaders, its foreign policy succeeded in this goal. By turning its back to the power politics and foreign wars of other nations, it could best show the revolutionary character of its new order and also demonstrate the peaceful achievements of this order, which, in turn, would impress and affect other nations. The temper underlying this attitude is still valid today, but under very different conditions; our new foreign policy still echoes George Washington's advice in his *Farewell Address*: "Observe good faith and justice towards all nations. . . . Nothing is more essential than that permanent, inveterate antipathies against particular nations and passionate attachments for others should be excluded and that, in place of them, just and amicable feelings toward all should be cultivated. . . . Though likewise a passionate attachment of one nation for another produces a variety of evils, sympathy for the favorite nation, facilitating the illusion of an imaginary common interest in cases where no real common interest exists and infusing into one the enmities of the other, betrays the former into a participation in the quarrels and wars of the latter without adequate inducement or justice."

Then, as now, "the supreme object of American foreign policy," as historian Charles A. Beard explained, was "to protect and promote the interests, spiritual and material, of the American people and, subject to that mandate, to conduct foreign affairs in such a manner as to contribute to the peace and civilization of mankind." Or, as Walter Lippmann described it, foreign policy was and is to be "the shield of the republic."

Before our entrance into the first world war, a policy strongly echoing early isolationism and warning against such participation was expressed by former President Theodore Roosevelt, who declared in September, 1914, that the United States had not "the smallest responsibility for what had happened to Belgium." "A deputation of Belgians has arrived in this country to invoke our assistance in the time of their dreadful need," he said, and continued, "It is certainly eminently desirable that we should remain entirely neutral and nothing but urgent need would warrant breaking our neutrality and taking sides one way or the other . . . and only the clearest and most urgent national duty would ever justify us in deviating from our rule of neutrality and non-interference."

The warning could still be heard as late as 1938, as, for instance, in General Hagood's testimony at the Naval Hearings: "I had been trying for forty-four years to find out what we were trying to do and have not been able to find out yet. The policy of the Navy is one thing, the policy of the Army is another thing and as far as I have ever been able to learn, the policy of the State Department is something else. . . . We should give up all idea of regulating the affairs of the world. . . . We should devote our entire attention to the problem of giving adequate and complete protection to our interests lying within the continental limits of the United States." But in 1941, as in 1915, despite such warnings, we entered a world war.

The full sweep of the adaptation of American doctrine from George Washington's time to our own was shown when President Harry S. Truman proclaimed on March 12, 1947: "I believe that it must be the policy of the United States to support peoples who are resisting attempted subjugation by armed minorities or by outside pressure. . . . Totalitarian regimes imposed upon free peoples by direct or indirect aggression undermine the foundations of international peace and hence the security of the United States." This doctrine came about while Greece defended herself in a desperate civil war against the Communist revolutionaries and while Turkey defended herself against heavy external pressure from the Soviets. Eisenhower's Middle East doctrine was proclaimed in the same vein, and our foreign policy now has many foreign commitments of this new kind.

What, then, is American foreign policy? To some degree, it depends upon who is defining it. As it seems to me, this stems from a confusion between the term "policy" and the term "doctrine." To me, foreign policy is a determining but frequently intangible generalization which acts as a guide, a collection of principles which form the basis for announced doctrines and for governmental operations as they apply to the needs of the time. Because the chief purpose of foreign policy is defense of the interests of the American people, it should be arrived at only after it has been determined just what the American people are willing to fight for.

For what will Americans fight? Will they fight for life? Of course, you say, they will fight to keep alive. That's the reason "Life" was one of the words written into the Declaration of Independence as one of the inalienable rights. But how can you get people to fight for what they already have and really have no fear of losing? Charles Sorenson, for many years a close associate of Henry Ford, Sr., expressed in a recent book a typical American point of view when he wrote: "I can not bring myself to fearing the Russians—having built plants in their land, having seen how incompetent the individuals are—I simply cannot fear these people as possible destroyers of such an advanced people as the Americans."

Will the American people fight for liberty? We have had liberty for two centuries, and the present generation, except for a limited number of recent escapees, is thoroughly unable even to imagine what it would mean to lose personal liberty, let alone natural liberty. Or will people perhaps fight for the right to pursue happiness? This, too, is not much of a ground on which to build. Though the psychologists are kept busy with psychopathic cases, most of the American people are happy and have the means of attaining increased happiness.

Will they fight, then, for high moral principles, perhaps to extend to others the privileges of life, liberty, and the pursuit of happiness? This is probably closer to the truth, since we are the greatest international Boy Scouts of all time. We have been willing to give to others more than sixty billion dollars to help them with their problems. Even today a high percentage of the American people like to think of themselves as great crusaders, as saviors of mankind, as knights riding to free the captive maiden. Former Ambassador George F. Kennan, in his book *Realities of American Policy,* mourns this spirit when he writes: "Americans seemed to lose their feeling for reality generally about foreign policy. A posture flowing strictly from the objects of our society as originally conceived ceased to satisfy them. Here, as in other respects, the romantic spirit seized them." If Mr. Kennan, a student and admirer of power politics in the style of Bismarck's *Realpolitik* (which never came out a winner in the end, though), seems to deplore this, he also seems to forget that a high moral objective, which is not necessarily "romantic," has always been a dominant force in doctrines and foreign policies of this country, even when these doctrines and policies were isolationist in different times. That there is no real contradiction was well shown by Ambassador Hugh Gibson, who remarked: "If we are to have a sound foreign policy, it must be realistic. It would be mistaken to consider this as a cynical attitude. If realism describes a policy that can be operated to achieve desirable results, there is nothing in it to exclude idealism. On the contrary, to be genuinely realistic, a policy must be lighted by idealism."

Yet it is perhaps merely a matter of taste and temperament, and rather vain at any rate, whether we stress the elements of idealism or those of realism in our foreign policy. In the long run, a good case can be made for the claim that our most altruistic policies have served our self-interest and therefore that our morality, which leads us to help others without cold calculations, turns out in the end to our own benefit. In short, it might well be that our enlightened egoism and our authentic altruism really stem from the same sources and lead to the same effects.

One way or the other, it would seem that our foreign policy cannot do without the following standards: First, it must have high moral purpose or it won't be supported by the American people. Second, its aim and doctrine must be formulated in simple terms or it won't be understood, and therefore not upheld, by the electorate. Third, it must be positive in its ultimate aims, like any other undertaking that counts on the support of peoples. Fourth, it must be progressive because this is the American way as seen by Americans and as others see it. Fifth, it must have short-term goals in addition to the long-term ones because Americans are a pragmatic and sometimes impatient people who want to strive for and see results tomorrow rather than in a distant future. Sixth, and not least, it must be practical. This is probably the most important maxim of American foreign policy, since it is inherent in the American character as well as in the nature of policies, foreign and otherwise. The truism that actions speak louder than words might be more precise if we say that our words must lead up to and conform with our actions. Whether in America or abroad, a policy which consists mainly of words and which is not backed up by actions or whose words contradict the real actions taken will not find any support. It will not arrive at its proclaimed goal. In fact, it will backfire. The most pressing, most difficult problem for American foreign policy, it seems to me, might well be the escape from our dilemma between words and actions. We must act in a way which confirms all those words which we loftily proclaim and in which we believe. In the reality presented by the situation of a foreign country or of a special measure, it is often less easy and takes more courage for us to live up to our own intentions than to act according to sloganized words and glittering generalizations.

Which of the doctrines, guiding principles, and goals which have shaped American foreign policy up to now remain valid and practicable in our day? Looking back, we find a long list of such doctrines. By the end of World War II it comprised, as given by Yale's Samuel Bemis in his *Diplomatic History of the United*

States, twelve main foreign-policy aims of the past. Starting with the doctrine of freedom of the seas, we moved next to the doctrine of freedom of commerce and navigation, or reciprocal equality of treatment without discrimination; then to isolationism, or abstention from the ordinary vicissitudes, coalitions, and collisions of European power politics and wars; further to the non-transfer principle of 1811, or opposition of transfer of adjacent European colonial dominions in the New World from one European sovereign to another; then to the manifest-destiny doctrine of continental expansion; on to the doctrine of self-determination of peoples; the Monroe Doctrine, opposing further European colonization in the new world; the doctrine of non-intervention in the internal affairs of other free nations; the doctrine of the right of expatriation and the wrong of impressment; suppression of the African slave trade; the good-neighbor doctrine of Pan-Americanism; and international arbitration by voluntary agreement.

If this was a quickly changing, sometimes contradictory, and mostly sensible sequence of reactions and demands in the American interest and tradition, an even longer, more quickly changing, more contradictory, and by no means always sensible sequence of new attitudes followed in the wake of World War II. Rather than policies based on our own interest and tradition, they were often mainly responses to the policies, tricks, and traps of the Soviets, who changed their line with the vigor of a whirling dervish. Its stages are marked by the policy subheads of appeasement, the Cold War, containment, and co-existence.

It has been my lot to watch these twists and turns of foreign policy from a vantage point where they were tested in their purest form—in the city of Berlin, divided between Allied and Soviet military occupants. Appeasement, the hang-over of wartime illusions in which the Soviets made us believe they were our friends and allies, was the guiding policy when I led the first road convoy through the Soviet Zone of Germany on June 17, 1945. Good will between East and West was celebrated in Vodka parties and boar hunts until the Westerners could not help discovering that it was as much of a myth as the planned joint four-power control

of Berlin itself. We found a Communist-dominated city government, which the Soviets had set up before our arrival and which
was completely subservient to them and indifferent to our desires.

As it became clear that Communist control of Berlin was
simply a model for the intended Communist control of Germany,
the Americans, British, and French began to insist upon a fair
share in the control of this city, a right which had been won on
the battlefield and by additional economic and political concessions. Directly before coming to Berlin, we had turned over to the
Soviet control the rich lands of Saxony and Thuringia, complete
with cattle in the fields and supplies in the warehouses. In return,
we had found our sectors of Berlin stripped by the Soviets of all
valuable things that could be driven out or torn up and moved
away.

By the spring of 1946, after hundreds of four-power conferences and daily contacts with the Soviet-appointed city government of Berlin, it was obvious that we were not supporting democracy but were backing Soviet intentions. The Western powers
were demanding that the Germans be given permission to hold
free elections, as had been promised at the four-power meeting
in July, 1945, at Potsdam. The election in Berlin on October 20,
1946, brought a thumping defeat to the Communist party; despite
their use of every trick, fair and foul, to win a majority, they got
only 20 per cent of the votes in the entire city. Soviet attempts
to win control of this elected new government provoked German
and Western resistance, which led directly to the blockade of
Berlin by the Soviet Union. Meanwhile, of course, the failure of
appeasement had become more and more obvious to all at various
international conferences in Moscow, London, and elsewhere.

We opposed the blockade of Berlin with the airlift, backed up
by the courageous German people and the Allies. But once we
had won the victory, we met with the Soviets in Paris and agreed
to a *status quo,* a divided city of Berlin, the continuation of a
divided Germany, and the implication that the Western powers
were willing to permit the Soviet Union to indulge in further use
of force to attain political and economic aims.

If this was officially termed "containment" by the then head of the State Department planning unit, George Kennan, co-existence was its real name: as long as we wouldn't surrender to the Soviets, we would permit them to run their part of the world while we would run ours and get along as best we could. But as the Berlin test proved, co-existence enabled the Soviets to have a base of operations against the West in East Berlin and to prepare a base for future operations against West Germany if and when Western influence could be diminished and Western troops made to leave. If this did not come to pass, it was only because those responsible for policy in Berlin understood the peril and were prepared to expose, against severe criticisms, the intent, as well as the activities, of the Communists.

In far-off Korea, co-existence broke down again, after American troops had been withdrawn from the south and after a blundering statement from our Secretary of State indicated that we would not return. With Russian backing, arms, and direction, the North Korean Communists moved southward as the first step in conquest. It was pretty obvious to anyone who would listen or hear or read that co-existence meant no existence for us. That Communism was a world conspiracy dedicated to our destruction was finally recognized by all except those under its spell.

Containment, as formulated by George Kennan, followed, although, in fact, it was already in effect globally in every place where we were defending ourselves, as best we could, against the political, economical, psychological, and, in some cases, military attacks of the Communists. Korea and Greece were good examples of the containment doctrine. We didn't prevent the hordes of Mao Tse-tung from gaining complete control of all of China, nor could we keep Indochina from losing great chunks of territory to the Communists. If containment was better than the two preceding policies, it didn't go far enough. It was a form of political Maginot Line thinking, a defensive concept which did not fit the situation, that is, the strategy of the enemy or the interests of the American people.

After Korea's dead were buried, after the French had lost Indochina, after the Soviets had managed to get absolute control over many millions of new slaves in these and other countries, we began to talk of a new policy, a policy of liberation. Yet it never got much beyond a state of hopeful words which encouraged satellites to throw off their Communist yokes and implied moral and material support from the West. When the East Berliners and East Germans rose up in the spirit of liberation in June, 1953, we betrayed their hope as we would do again in Hungary three years later. All liberation talk was quashed by American willingness to return to the conference table and sit down with Communist perpetrators of past and present crimes. From Berlin to Geneva was just a jump from one conference table to another, where the Soviets succeeded in proving that our new doctrine consisted only of words; in reality, we smiled at the Soviets rather than liberating their victims; we strengthened the Soviet leaders rather than their captive peoples.

We found ourselves back in a policy of appeasement, but a cautious appeasement this time, promising to let bygones be bygones if the Soviets would, in the future, not act like Communists. In back of this cautious appeasement was the oft-expressed Western threat of massive retaliation. This policy had its good points, but it lost most of them when the Soviets perfected their atomic and hydrogen bombs, so that massive retaliation became a two-edged sword. With its partial loss, we became even more willing—though still showing reluctance—to give in to Soviet demands on and from the summit, well aware of the evil consequences, yet at the same time beset by vague hopes.

What, then, are the factors which shape our foreign policy today? With the world situation being what it is, our policies seem determined in the main by two factors: first, America's popular mood of the moment and second, America's leadership. The two factors supplement each other; sometimes the first, and then again the second, is in the lead, yet there is no contradiction between them.

The popular attitude of a vast majority of the people of the United States today can well be expressed as a preference for peace, plenty, and postponement. Peace we want because we're fed up with wars and preparation for wars. "Force" has almost become a dirty word, if not tantamount to reprehensible, uncouth violence. Though we recognize the need of discipline in the home, of policemen in the streets, and of sailors on our ships, we strongly dislike force and are even more strongly opposed to war. World Wars I and II and Korea have disillusioned the American people. The man in uniform, with some exceptions, has been deliberately deflated, his pride pricked, his conceit shrunk. Today, many men in the armed forces do not at all feel their service to be a glorious distinction; rather, they see themselves as displaced civilians. This feeling is not entirely new among Americans. It was already popular to ridicule the Reserve Officers Training Corps in my college days of the early twenties. At the time, leading American magazines carried advertisements over the banner of "World Peaceways," with such headings as "SUCKER" showing crippled veterans of the first world war as a warning against military service. "Wars are produced by ammunition makers for the sake of profit," said a best-selling book of the time, and this idea prevailed among the "intelligentsia." Today, the man or woman who expresses patriotic sentiment is frequently and sneeringly denounced as a superpatriot or a chauvinist by the Fancy Dans of the world of words. To wave a flag, despite the worthy efforts of the American Legion, remains an action which would embarrass most. All the glories and illusions and glamour of war, viewed with the disillusioned eye of this atomic age, are as bare as a freshly plucked deep-freeze turkey. Therefore, if the premise of foreign policy is based upon those things for which a people will fight and die, we must concede that the American people will not fight and die for the sake of war itself. Conversely, while they accept unhesitatingly and with open arms the joys of peace, it is not at all certain that they recognize the need to fight for peace.

Plenty we have. Never has the proverbial horn of plenty spilled more goods into the American kitchen, even in moments of "recession." Farm production is still at surplus levels. Twenty-two million tons of corn and wheat are still in storage in government warehouses. Factories and foundries sing merrily all the day long. New cars, pleasure cars, luxury cars, roll off the assembly line to the tune of over 6,000,000 a year. So great is their abundance, so fast their production that 5,700,000 homes have at least two cars in the garage. The competition to get rid of them is so keen that sometimes the decisive element determining sales is the size of meaningless tail fins.

Even after taxes, the remaining individual income of most every citizen goes far compared to that of any other worker in the world. Our industry creates enough surplus to expend approximately fifty billion dollars a year in plant expansion and improvement. There are over seventy million American men and women working right now, and working, in the vast majority of cases, for the production of consumer goods. These goods include everything from steel girders for new buildings to deep-freeze iceboxes.

We are so prosperous that we can even afford to junk valuable airplanes and substitute new ones, to build whole fleets of the new all-jet B-52 bombers at a cost of eight million dollars each. Gadgetry is more than a vogue; it is a craze in America. We have man-made sunlamps, dog bootees, pens that write under water, shirts that are automatically pressed on their dryers, watches that need no winding, and cans that cook their contents without external heat, 48,651,070 television sets, two hundred million radios—all produced not for a limited few but for an entire population. Of all production in the United States, approximately 64 per cent is consumer goods, while only 10 per cent can be considered as going into war preparation materials. In Russia, the reverse holds true.

In addition to the desire for peace and the enjoyment of plenty, there is a third reason why Americans tend to postpone their decision to fight in any form: no one appears to know the perfect answer to the problems of the world or the right course of action to overcome them. We have tried to buy friendship and have gained only scorn. We have been enraged by Tito's shooting down unarmed American planes, only to see him at the receiving end of economic aid and military assistance by the United States a couple of years later. We have heard the international cry of "Wolf! Wolf!" until we no longer care. We have heard the government and the people of America being insulted and scorned by the Communists until we have placidly accepted their insults. We hardly bother about the degradation of American citizens in foreign countries and about the imprisonment of American citizens without trial. All these things we now take for granted as they are "played down" by our leaders. This betrays a calming influence, a cooling off of our emotions, a substitution of reason for feeling which might be salutory. But what is bad about it is that it may signal the beginning decay of the patriotic spirit of a great people.

If you believe this appeal to cold reasoning is to the good, let me ask you a few questions. If the American people had decided their course of action only upon a rational basis, would we have fought World War I for freedom of the seas or, as Woodrow Wilson said later, "to make the world safe for democracy"? Would we have fought World War II had we not been emotionally stirred by the horrors of Hitler's Third Reich?

I faced this question in a dramatic form in 1945, at the end of the second world war. My job in Berlin, and in France before that, had been, as a military government officer, to attempt to restore the destroyed cities and peoples left in the wake of our advancing armies. I had seen enough destruction, suffering, starvation, and shattered lives to jump at the first opportunity to visit Switzerland. Here was a neat, clean, compact little country with beautiful mountains, lovely valleys, hospitable people, and intact democratic institutions. Around it had washed the fury of war, yet in this cool, safe spot there was only peace and wealth and well-being. "Why," I asked myself, "can't we Americans be like the Swiss? Why must we travel to foreign lands every twenty years, participate in the hell of war, disrupt our economy, and brutalize our feelings?" My answer was that Americans are like no one except Americans. We have been guided in our great policies more by emotions than by cold reason. Is this good or is this bad? Would you want us to be indifferent to the plight of hapless Jews being burned in the ovens of Buchenwald?

Think, for a moment, of an everyday incident in our midst. When a speeding truck was bearing down upon a small child playing in the street, a man in the full vigor of twenty-five years rushed out, threw the child to safety, and was killed himself. Was he a fool or was he a hero to be admired or pitied? You might reason that a family lost a father and breadwinner, while the government lost an individual in whom it had invested the expenses of education in twenty-five years of growth, whereas the child was still only a small investment and for many, many years would be only an expense before reaching the man's position of benefit to the state. Yet if quite a good cause can be made out rationally to prove that the man was a fool, I will not accept it. How would the American majority judge it?

This is by no means a far-fetched example. Surely the Communists would declare the man a fool, as I had reason to learn from a similar problem in the early days of the occupation of Berlin. At the time, the people of the city were starving, with a third of the population of more than three million trying to live on eleven hundred calories a day; they were popularly known as those in the starvation category. When a small amount of additional food could be brought to the city, the question was debated at the Berlin Allied Kommandatura whether it should be allotted to undernourished, sickly children or go, by way of plant distribution, to laborers in the factories; it would enable them to produce more goods. The American, British, and French view was in favor of the children, while the Soviet view, as expressed by Soviet General Alexander Kotakov, favored the grown workers, although they were already receiving almost three thousand calories of food a day.

As it looks to me, if we get rid of our American emotions, we will lose ourselves and our America. But as we view the popular temper, it apparently does not agree at all with this "rational," heartless, immoral attitude. George Kennan to the contrary notwithstanding, it is "romantic" rather than *realpolitisch*. This temper shapes our foreign policy as much as the tendency toward peace, plenty, and postponement.

We also find this temper reflected in our leadership, particularly in Dwight D. Eisenhower. Even his enemies, for all men have some, concede that he and his actions are almost perfect reflections of the desires of a vast majority of the American people. His dominating traits are calm moderation and balance as it comes from travel on the middle of the road. His forbearance and avoidance of extremes is reminiscent of the tolerance shown by Abraham Lincoln when the radical Republicans opposed his policy of temporizing with the South. While they favored all-out war against the South, taking over estates and property of the Southerners, dividing the land among the Negroes, freeing the slaves immediately, and crushing the secessionists for all time, Lincoln opposed it; and so would Eisenhower.

True, the popular clichés which express Eisenhower's attitude and his policies can be answered by equally valid opposite clichés. "Don't rock the boat" has as a counterpart: "If you don't, you'll drift over the falls." Or "Always leave the door open" is contradicted by "The burglars can come in." If "diplomacy by personal charm" suggests that smiles are an asset, "business is business." A course of "no extremes" is countered by the philosopher Hegel's "Nothing great in the world has been accomplished without passion."

Never has a President been more ideally suited to reflect and to carry out the will of the American people in a world of confusion. Eisenhower is no extremist; America fears extremists. He is no eccentric genius; America distrusts eccentricity. He is no head-in-the-clouds zealot; America suspects zealots. His love of moderation is as balanced as a statement by Sir Roger de Coverly in Addison's *The Spectator*: "There is much to be said on both sides of the question." America trusts this man. His wide grin, his homey platitudes, his let's-keep-our-shirts-on point of view seems to the average American voter a mirror of his own point of view. He seems to be an average American employing ordinary common sense.

Eisenhower has brought the dignity of George Washington to the office of President. He has given to government officials clear responsibilities and has achieved comparative efficiency of operation. If he has time to play golf or to fish, this is proof that his organization is functioning. No one man can run the American government or any one part of it. It is vital that a President recognize his limitations.

It is obvious that there have been great postponements of decisions at Washington. "Delay is preferable to error," Jefferson wrote to George Washington in 1792. Eisenhower has preferred to postpone decisions until all facts are in, and in many of the world situations today, to get all facts is impossible, except on a piecemeal basis; only then can the pros and cons be summed up. There are many problems in the world which cannot be decided from Washington and it is high time that someone had courage enough to say so. Where Eisenhower hesitates, it's his decision not to decide; 2,876,439 men in the land, sea, and air forces representing five countries were co-ordinated and directed by him in a manner far beyond the competence of any Napoleon or Alexander the Great. No average man could have achieved this feat—as little as the co-ordination and direction of thousands of bombers, blinking their lights from horizon to horizon in the May night skies of England or of infantry divisions moving into action at Saint-Lô, France, with ambulances meeting trains on time and vast tonnages of supplies crossing the beaches at Cherbourg. To succeed in all of this in accordance with the political concepts of forty-eight nations and to destroy one of the greatest military forces ever assembled is proof of an organizing and executive genius which cannot be brushed aside by "intellectuals" who prefer wisecracks to wisdom, phrases to feats, and words to actions.

The federal government is probably better organized and commanded today than during any time of its existence. It has become hard and efficient, but this can be bad as well as good. Americans have never fully trusted government or governmental wisdom. An efficient government with wrong aims and direction is indeed a dangerous thing, but an inefficient government in world affairs can be even more dangerous. The American people will back President Eisenhower's decisions because they believe in him.

The middle-of-the-road policy, which Eisenhower embraced by temperament, is the common denominator of American domestic and foreign policy. Both at home and abroad, it shuns extremes and tends toward the compromise. Its efficiency and its shortcomings, its failures and successes, its achievements and its problems can only be tested and judged on the spot. It is contradictory, piecemeal and opportunistic. In terms of law, it is based on the case-history method, which is also the method of English common law. It is not the law of an over-all, rigid, all-encompassing code of a Napoleon but, rather, the "good way" of Buddha or, more precisely, the pragmatic, step-by-step common-sense way of America.

An opponent has said that this policy of America is like a man who trusts in God, has dreams in his head, love in his heart, economic aid in his left hand, and military punch in his right. He travels down the middle of the road which leads to an unknown destination, trying to please everybody. Too frequently, he gives economic aid to his enemies and punches his friends. Perhaps the best answer to such a critic had been given by Old Bill, whom some of us remember as the famous cartoon personality of World War I. Old Bill and his pal were in a shell hole in No Man's Land, a really bad hot spot, with shells coming in from all directions. Bill's pal was saying what a bad hole they were in. Bill's answer was: "If you know a better 'ole, get along to it."

This American foreign policy was not my way, nor was it the way of all the others who, from 1945 on, favored economic and political showdowns with the Soviet Union in order to force a termination of the threat of war. At that time, we had the atomic bomb and a decisive voice in the world, even though we had disbanded, if not thrown away, our military might at the end of the second world war while the Soviet Union built up its strength to intimidate and finally conquer us. At that time, many of us were denounced as warmongers rattling the saber and charged with antagonism toward our great wartime ally. But as a fair observer must admit today, we could have compelled the Soviet Union at the time, between 1945 and 1950, to live up to its agreements; we could have put into effect measures to prevent and outlaw the very type of world war which we now fear. In 1950, I wrote in my book *Berlin Command*: "Will the democratic nations of the world permit Russia, who has repeatedly announced her intention to destroy us, our government and our way of life, to accumulate this new means of annihilating us?" It was the last moment to do so, and it was not done.

Russia now has the new means of annihilating us—not only the atom bomb but the hydrogen bomb and the means of delivering them. However, we Americans do not believe in recriminations and rather dislike the saying "I told you so." But we must learn from our mistakes. We must not be afraid to threaten with our superior force if and when the enemy wants to overpower us with his force because he expects us not to defend ourselves. Unless we use our power, he will strike first. This is the sort of a situation I assume was envisioned by the Secretary of State when he referred to "these perilous times."

3 Ghana: New Nation in the Making

In Ghana, white men try awfully hard to please black men. Although white people are not allowed to own property, they are most welcome if, when, and as long as they behave themselves. As a matter of fact, even when they do misbehave, the black judge shows great tolerance for their weaknesses. When they are guilty of, say, speeding, he is likely merely to explain the rules to them, with the kindly admonition: "Please, do not do this again." This may seem to many Americans like having the shoe on the other foot. This former Gold Coast colony, which has become a sovereign, independent nation of the British Commonwealth since 1957, is "colored" from top to bottom. Its people are the most erect-walking men and women in the world, bright and happy in their toga-like, gay-colored gowns. They have cheerful dispositions, and their drive to get ahead in the world seems to outspace their ability to adjust themselves to a new life.

Although Ghana has the air of Africa at its darkest, I sensed something very British in all of it. For here, British colonialism has done a great job and has earned a debt of gratitude which, though never paid, will nonetheless exist in the memories and activities of these free men for centuries. The fine roads, the smartly uniformed soldiers, the clipped British accents, and the surprising brevity of speech suggest British influence. Behind, around, and over Ghana's atmosphere hovers the great British tradition of gentlemanly dignity. This dignity has certain drawbacks, however. White wigs on the Ghanian judges look a bit out of place in their country. Since British authority is associated with a big house in the suburbs, the present rulers have taken over what they call the "estate houses," thereby drawing fire from opposition forces in the Ghana Parliament.

Although the British went to the Gold Coast more than a hundred years ago, they didn't really buckle down to the job of developing it until the last sixty years of their rule. They could start peaceful work only after they had successfully defeated the war-minded Ashanti tribes, which for almost a hundred years had fought and harassed the British and their native allies, the coastal tribes of the Fantis and the Ewes. The fighting wasn't all one sided; one military governor, Sir Charles McCarthy, had his head made into a royal Ashanti drinking cup in 1824.

In their "creative colonialization," the British had a long-range plan of training the Ghanians for independence; once they arrived at this goal, the British would gradually withdraw their controls and welcome the Gold Coast into the British Commonwealth. They termed this their method of "planned abdication," but scheduling got booted about a bit during recent years, with the result that independence was granted before the British felt that the natives were ready for it.

On time or not, the natives were led into the independent stage by a fabulous character, Kwame Nkrumah. At present Ghana's prime minister, Nkrumah is the son of a poor native goldsmith who lives in a mud hut. He was educated at British-installed schools; after graduation, he came to study in the United States, first at Lincoln University, where he gained his bachelor's degree in theology, and then at the University of Pennsylvania. During his ten years in the United States, his interests shifted from theology and abstract scholarship to politics. He became determined to lead his people to complete independence and the opportunities which would thereby be granted them. "If I fail to bring self-government to the Gold Coast, bury me alive!" he wrote home to one of his friends. How to accomplish his aims was an open question. He found a few answers while at the University of London, where he studied economics and became adept at practical politics. "How to make trouble for the powers in control," an unofficial yet effective class, seems to have led the list of his studies in the latter field, and he learned how to use it in his later studies of Communism.

It seems natural that upon his return to the Gold Coast Nkrumah would apply the techniques of mob psychology, authority-baiting, and elaborate promises in words, all of which he had learned to master. It was also natural that the British authorities would throw this troublemaker into the hoosegow. This they promptly did in 1950 on charges of a rather general nature close to sedition and stirring up disorder. But in response to these disorders and to the fire they set to the hearts of the black men of the Gold Coast, the British chose to investigate the conditions which had provoked the unrest; the outcome was a strong recommendation for a greater degree of freedom. When the political jailbird's party, the Convention People's party, overwhelmingly won an election, the British, with their usual magnanimity, forgave Nkrumah's sins and freed him to head both his party and a new government. Today, Nkrumah, apparently an intelligent, well-meaning man, recognizes his obligation to the British, as well as the great opportunity that is now open for his people.

The Communists have been making a play in Ghana, but the play is not even in the same ball park with the real game. Although at the independence ceremonies on March 6, 1957, the Soviets were represented by a delegation, although they have, possibly for political purposes, made one large purchase of cocoa, and although they have suggested, for their own political gain, an exchange of ambassadors, they have made little headway. The problems faced by this new government as it tries to push the advancement of its people are serious enough without the interference of the Kremlin.

Ghana's first need is for outside help. This has been publicly acknowledged by the Prime Minister, and steps are being taken to recruit such assistants who will work as aids to the present Ghana government rather than foreign overlords of the government. However, getting expert aid is easier said than done. Ghana isn't too inviting a land for white guests—muggy at times, then again, terribly hot, in short, the tropics. A century ago, the country was known as the white man's graveyard; when whites came to get slaves for America before the traffic was stopped, they often died. Of twenty-four Danish governors ruling the Gold Coast in the brief span from 1700 to 1750, when Denmark owned that land, only four survived its climate to return to their homeland alive.

Other foreign nations ruled the Gold Coast—before the Danes, the Portuguese, and long before the Portuguese, the Carthaginians. These hardy North Africans who, two thousand years ago, used to sail down the west coast of Africa to what later became known as the Gold Coast, developed an extraordinary form of trade with the natives, the so-called "dumb trade." The Carthaginians, anchored off the coast, would send longboats ashore, where their crews would build bonfires. After leaving various things which they had for sale—beads, colored cloth, and other items likely to attract the natives—they returned to their boats for the night. In the morning, they returned to the spot and found beside the goods a quantity of gold dust. If the price offered pleased them, they left the goods and returned with the gold dust to their ship. But if the quantity of gold dust did not satisfy them, they left both goods and payment for another night. During the night, the natives would again sneak out to the beach; when they saw their dust still lying around, they either put up more of it as an offer or left the goods and took their gold along with them. The next morning, the Carthaginians came ashore again, either to take the larger amount of gold dust and leave the goods for the natives or to leave the gold dust and return to their ship with the goods.

Methods of trading in Ghana have changed, but they still seem strange enough. Take, for instance, Ghana's so-called "mammy trade," which I observed as it is carried on in all of the big markets at Accra. Mammy, usually a buxom entrepreneur, carries in her head the detailed trade exchanges and transactions taking place in her market stalls for weeks and months. She is reputed to be able to remember accurately the day-by-day accounts of a dozen clients and a turnover of goods involving up to $1,000 without errors, ever.

What makes the mammy trade so significant is that it results from the lack of elementary education of the Ghanians, which is still prevalent even today. If a mammy has prospered and sends her bright son through school and up to college at the University of Ghana, or even to Oxford, she expects him to come back with a knowledge of all those things that will make her business even more profitable and her prestige more outstanding. Although she cannot point it out, she needs someone familiar with the system of double-entry bookkeeping to make her business modern and up to date. But what her son brings back from the University is a knowledge of Plato and quotations from Aristotle. His ambition is no longer to run a market but to be a white-collar man able to use all those words that are associated with a real gentleman of the old school. One of Ghana's chief problems, then, is her need of practical training and applied education to bridge the gap between the existing elementary schools and the important, though impractical, academic studies of the classicists.

Education is closely related to another problem which Prime Minister Nkrumah and his associates must cope with: the economic betterment of their people. To get into power, Nkrumah could mainly stick to the lyrics of a popular American song: "I can do anything better than you can—yes, I can, yes I can, yes I can." But now that he is in power, he must fulfill his promises; to do so, he has already expressed his very sensible willingness to welcome outside assistance in the form of technical aid and financial support. But the real problem for him is to attract to this difficult land the necessary technical help.

What is needed are incentives for foreign aid. Patriotism used to be an incentive, as was the lust for adventure. The British, notoriously patriotic and eternally adventurous, are, perhaps, still his best prospects, for it is said that for ten thousand dollars a year, a first-rate English engineer can be obtained, whereas double that price would probably fail to interest a really good American engineer. Another incentive for attracting help, religion, still leads to efficient results. The Methodists, the Presbyterians, and now, vigorously, the Catholics are engaged in running hospitals, schools, and libraries for the benefit of the people of Ghana. These devoted souls are quite willing, for little or no pay, to sacrifice their lives for uplifting the retarded children of God. Profitable trade is the third and best incentive. The original exploitation of the Gold Coast was based upon trade in the products of its soil, from gold dust to slaves to cocoa, which is still Ghana's major product. When foreign firms send their technical experts, they may benefit by profitable trade with Ghana.

One of the main prerequisites of all this, and a decisive third problem before present-day Ghana, is to create a strong central government able to plan and carry through the evolution. But the concept of a strong central government clashes head on with the century-old tribal system based upon family groupings and loyalty to the tribal chieftains. The Ashantis, particularly, resist central control. The whole struggle recalls England's eleventh-century struggle which the pre-Norman Saxons, who favored great decentralization of authority, led against the Normans, who thought in terms of high concentration of centralized power. It is quite possible that in this struggle at Ghana, the result will be the same as it was in England, that is, a compromise.

The British respected Ghana's tribal customs and were very slow to force change. The present government, with all the cocksureness of modern planners, is determined to change everything from family loyalty to the clothing of the natives. "We will have decentralized district assemblies working with the central government," one of the ministers of Ghana told me, "and the tribal chieftains will either have to go along with modern developments or be left behind." Since 90 per cent of the people of Ghana live in the bush, are illiterate, and cling to their traditions, the other 10 per cent, mostly city-dwellers, who do take an interest in modern government, face a rough job in bringing about this modernization.

Fortunately, Ghana knows no food problems. No one is hungry, which makes Ghana a rich country in one sense. The prevalent diet of maize, yams, coconuts, and vegetables is more than adequate. But a difficulty arises for the leaders in their attempts to maintain a balanced budget because Ghana's economy is too closely tied to the export of cocoa, which accounts for two-thirds of Ghana's entire exports. When the world price was more than £400 per ton, the cocoa raisers and the government never had it so good. In 1957, however, when the price fell to a little over £150 per ton, everybody was in trouble. The government had guaranteed the growers a minimum price of £150 per ton and had an unavoidable additional expense of £50 per ton for shipping, handling, and other charges. Therefore, the reserve funds of the government were diminished, and the welfare activities of the government, as well as the developments of state planning, were curtailed. With prices again on the upturn, the economic stability of Ghana is also improving. But even with satisfactory world prices, menaces remain; a cocoa-tree disease known as "swollen shoots" necessitates the weeding out of thousands of infected trees so that they will not kill the healthy ones.

The greatest danger to the good people of Ghana, however, is not swollen shoots or local politics or foreign imperialism. It is the very real threat that Nkrumah, unable to accomplish flashy success at home, may reactivate the Communist-inspired dream of his London student days: a quickly attained union of all Africa, brought about by violence, with its accompanying suffering and chaos, rather than through the orderly hard work of self-improvement. Nkrumah's strange union of Ghana with Guinea; his crackdown on Ghana's legislative body; his sponsorship of the screaming All Africa Peoples' Conference held at Accra in December, 1958; his public friendship with such Communist-trained rabblerousers as Tom Mboya, Jomo Kenyatta, Sekou Touré, and others like them—these straws in the wind may foretell Nkrumah's tragic loss of moderation and his acceptance of the destructive force of hate.

What do we Americans and our foreign policy have to do about all this? I'd say we don't *have* to do anything. These problems and opportunities belong to the independent sovereign state of Ghana. True, on a private level, American businessmen can do business with Ghana's businessmen, American missionaries can go there in quest of souls, and the more hardy American tourists may go there for very unusual, often bizarre, sensations.

The United States can be enticed to give aid on occasion, although hardly for imperative interests of its own security. Ghana is far from Russia's borders, and Communism does not appeal to the strong individualism of the citizen of Ghana. Our government can also continue to keep up its first-class American Embassy to do honor to the new government, to observe, to advise. It can also keep open in Ghana the doors of one of the most effective United States Information Agency offices in existence. It shows a marked contrast to the British information office, with its great dignity; the way the British office operates, it seems to tell the natives: "Make yourself worthy to come into this fine building and to be among gentlemen." But the American information office, located on the second floor of an old building in the center of the teeming, throbbing, stinking Accra market, tries hard to reach the masses. When I visited it last, I counted more than 120 men of Ghana reading books, periodicals, and newspapers about America, all this being supervised and skillfully controlled by Dr. Sawyer, an American Negro.

America can also arrange to send representatives, or goodwill ambassadors, to visit Ghana on occasion, as did Vice-President Nixon at the birth of this nation on March 6, 1957. "It is a tribute to the leaders of Ghana and the United Kingdom," said Vice-President Nixon, "that your independence has been achieved in orderly fashion. . . . The future is indeed bright for Ghana." Mr. Nixon's old-fashioned, handshaking American politicking (according to Ghana rumors, he even handed out fountain pens and pencils) turned out to make a tremendous hit with the ordinary people of Ghana but not with the British, who believe in a high degree of decorum and dignity, nor with the more elevated intelligentsia of Ghana. Mr. Nixon may well have pointed the way for America's role at Ghana, as well as in other parts of the world, by appealing to the common man. If this be done in cooperation with the British, who tend to encourage the cultivation of the uncommon man, an efficient division of labor will occur.

In brief, American foreign policy in the new Republic of

Ghana, where no U.S. security interests are at stake, may well leave that country's development to its new leaders. American free enterprise and free associations may build bridges, but as a nation, we can and should remain detached, friendly bystanders. Whether their "freedom from the colonial power" has brought much good to the Ghanians remains a very open question, but now that they have it, we can wish them well and hope that they will proceed under their own steam.

4 Belgian Congo: Old-Fashioned Colony

In the back country of the Belgian Congo, feathered, painted, pulsating, wriggling men and women are still beating their drums, and in doing so, they make our rational twentieth-century civilization seem a shade less certain. Maybe these pagans sense a few things which we are only learning now. They used a mildew to cure infection before we discovered penicillin, and their witch doctors guard secret formulas which often work medical miracles. When I was in a village in the Upper Congo, a woman died in childbirth. Her mother went into the jungle, drank a witch brew, and was then able to nurse the orphan baby to full life. A friend told me of a man of the cloth who had stopped at his farm on a big-game hunt. Eight days later and sixty miles away, the man was killed by an elephant he thought he had shot to death. Within an hour, the jungle drums had carried the message back to my friend. The location given was so accurate that my friend could leave immediately and recover the body. How had the drums carried the story? There is no written or oral explanation of the power of the jungle drums. In the Congo, you hear of many cases of black magic in the pagan jungle. Could it be that the zombie souls of departed relatives play through native minds as realistically as the spirit of the Holy Ghost plays through the minds of advanced Christians?

The Belgian Congo is the heart of Africa. It seems to consist of jungle, rain forests, copper-mining communities, the fast-growing metropolis of Leopoldville, and people who are evolving under a strict Belgian paternal system. Henry M. Stanley, who finally started his famed pursuit of David Livingstone in 1871, was so impressed by the country that he tried to get Great Britain interested. Failing this, he convinced Leopold II of Belgium that he should take over, and this the King did—for his own private benefit. Hippopotamus whips cracked over the backs of the unwilling natives. Wealth poured in for Leopold, and so did the criticism of a shocked nation. From Leopold's days to ours, the Belgian Congo has undergone great physical and philosophical changes. The land that Livingstone didn't like when he moved on to the Lake Tanganyika area is liked by many today. Livingstone had said: "Everything for the Nile, but I'll not be made into black man's meat for the Congo." A Belgium businessman in the Upper Congo told me: "We'll do everything we can for these backward people to help them in their development, but we won't let ourselves be pushed by the Communists, nor by a few local agitators who wear the respectable clothes of civilization and quote modern philosophers, but who understand nothing." Since America is reported to be "anti-colonial," many of the Belgian colonists are "anti-American."

One-third the size of the United States, the Belgian Congo is eight times the size of Belgium, its guiding father. The country has a valuable asset in pure copper, and today, more than five thousand small businesses exist. Some uranium is shipped out, manganese and cobalt are mined, and industrial diamonds, of which the Congo is the world's largest export country, are still abundant. Yet the greatest wealth of the Congo is the potential of its people. As elsewhere in Africa, "there is no wealth nor strength but in man."

Fifty thousand whites, of whom 75 per cent are Belgians, must help ten million blacks to raise their standard of living, change their pattern of thinking, and build up their communal lives in a world of fast communications. Some responsible Belgians calculate that this will take thirty years for the ten million people of the Belgian Congo and the four million in the United Nations trusteeship, Ruanda-Urundi. The agencies that the Belgians count upon to do the job are the Belgian governmental authorities, the Church, and big business. Right now, the state is footing the financial bill, the Church is supplying the unifying force and education, and big business is helping with the economic where-withal and promoting the development of community living, par-ticularly in the cities and in the vicinities of the great mining developments.

The Belgian Congo system is paternal, aimed at keeping eco-nomic, social, and political progress in interlocking balance. This appears in marked contrast to the highly developed political sys-tems directly across the Congo in French-controlled West Africa. As a local wisecracker explained to me: "Across the river where the French are, they have the privilege of free speech and the right to vote. On this side of the river the natives don't talk so much, but they eat better and live better." This situation pleases the Belgians; what the natives think of it is hard to tell. A thou-sand years ago, the natives had their own convictions and cul-ture. They still have their own convictions, but it would seem foolish for a white man to claim exact knowledge of what these convictions actually are. One thing seems certain: many of the native black men of the Congo prefer their old way of life to the supposedly new ideas of the modern world. In fact, their old way of life was not without its greatness. Before Portugal started its explorations in the fifteenth century, the natives had great leaders of their own. Before the slave trade developed exports to the United States, the art of the African mask successfully created the expressions of fear, love, and ecstasy. They had their wise men, such as Shamba Bolongongo, who introduced political, social, and moral reforms to the land. He restrained tribal vio-lence and ruled out knife-throwing (*shongo*): "Kill neither man, woman nor child," taught he. "Are they not the children of the god Chembe? And have they not the right to live?"

Inevitably, however, the people of the Congo are going to be modernized. So say the Belgians, at least, who have drawn up an elaborate ten-year plan. It sounds good to a Westerner, but there are some flies in the ointment, too. Great costs are involved in changing the ways of this population, 85 per cent of which lives in the bush and is backwards intellectually, as well as materially, by our standards. They're also short of vitality because of the heat. Maybe with air-conditioning there would be more energy and drive, but this would also require expensive electricity.

The ten-year plan to modernize the Belgian Congo will cost from $500,000,000 to $2,000,000,000. The Belgians claim to have invested $1,750,000,000 in it already. The new plan calls for $30,000,000 for the agricultural program; $40,000,000 for housing; $20,000,000 for drinking water; $40,000,000 for education; $40,000,000 for various kinds of training; $20,000,000 for airfields; $120,000,000 for roads. Raising this money is a much tougher job than that of the missionaries who went to the Congo to save souls and frequently settled for a Mother Hubbard. Former Belgian Minister of Colonies P. Wigny says that this one-billion-dollar development plan represents more than the total money distributed through international channels. He didn't say so, but I'm sure he did not have in mind the $60,000,000 directly distributed to backward and less backward areas by the United States.

How to attract financial investments is one of the Congo's major problems. To help in this direction, the Belgians have been placing advertisements in American newspapers. Signed "Inforcongo," they attempt to explain to the American people what the Belgians are doing in the Congo and what they would like to do. Of their paternal attitude they say: "In fact, there is no real democracy without two fundamental elements: First, a population capable of knowing wisely what it wants and organizing in such a way that it can verify whether or not its leaders are carrying out its will correctly. Second, elites capable of governing —that is, able to enlighten these populations." Of those natives in the process of evolution they say: "Most certainly the *Evolue* is not the native who has managed to imitate his civilizer more or less successfully, yet always superficially, but rather the individual human being who, by means of a long and close period of contact with the civilizer, acquires real intellectual maturity." What the Belgians are really trying to say is this: "We've got a plan, and we're doing the best we can. What we need is more of your financial investments to help us out and rather less of your verbal advice and interference." In Belgian eyes, the advice frequently comes from the United States, while the interference comes from the masterful wire-pullers of the Kremlin, who work through Indian and other Oriental agencies in an active underground to destroy the authorities of the state, the Church, and industry.

One of the brightest recent achievements in the Belgian Congo has been the work of the World Health Organization in making that country inhabitable for its native population, as well as for foreigners. The present tremendous industrial and housing development of Leopoldville would be impossible without this organization's help. In 1950, it traced the cause of filariasis (river blindness), a disease that was blinding both whites and blacks and sapping the vitality of the population, to certain insects originating from eggs deposited in the rapids of the Congo River. Once the source of the disease was discovered, a mixture of oil and DDT (dichloro-diphenyl-trichloro-ethane) was sprayed over the rapids, and the epidemic was effectively terminated.

A second, currently developing Louvain University merits credit for its introduction of higher practical education and tolerant integration to the Belgian Congo. It is the creation of its extraordinary rector, Monsieur le Chanoine L. Gillon. Until 1950, he was one of Belgium's outstanding nuclear physicists. How he learned I was coming to the Congo, I don't know, but he met me at the plane, took me to the newly created University, served lunch, and explained the extraordinary growth of education and tolerance in the Congo. The University buildings, when completed, will cost between fourteen and sixteen million dollars, 80 per cent of which will be supplied by the government. The rest must come from the gifts of industries interested in the welfare of the Congo, from foundations, and from men of philanthropic inclinations.

The Belgian Congo is a country our foreign policy can keep out of; in fact, it ought to keep out. Anti-colonialism alienates the Belgians without helping the natives. What helps both—and this is a help we can well provide—is industrial investment, where it is warranted, according to the standards of free enterprise, but only if and when it is of mutual profit to the Congo as well as to the American investors. We will not help anyone, least of all the natives, with irritating, aimless slogans of anti-colonialism, words which lead to actions that hurt our own interest and security. Modernization, stepped up at a quicker pace than the natives and their culture can bear, will only impose indigestible new forms on old values.

5 Kenya: Subversion in the Jungle

Jomo Kenyatta from Kenya and Kwame Nkrumah from the Gold Coast were pals in London. Both had been trained in the same Communist techniques, and both were determined to return to their respective countries, throw out the white man, and lead their people to a better life. Jomo was better prepared for this undertaking. He had studied Marxism and Communist teachings in Russia in 1929, 1932, and 1933 while staying at Moscow's Lux Hotel, the luxury dorm for the most outstanding students of the Comintern. When Nkrumah was secretary of the Fifth Pan-African Congress in London in 1945, Jomo was president. Moscow was a good school for both, and ample proof that they were good students of Communism can be seen in the techniques they used upon returning to their respective homelands. Yet in 1959, when Nkrumah was famous and victorious as prime minister of the newly created sovereign member-republic of the British Commonwealth, the Republic of Ghana, Jomo Kenyatta was a disgraced flop serving the first years of a seven-year sentence at hard labor. He has flunked his great opportunity. White men still rule his homeland, eleven thousand of his followers have been killed and thirty thousand captured, and his own people have turned against him.

This is a case study in success and failure of Communist subversion. Jomo's brilliant plan failed because the native black population of Kenya was not ready for it. Although the people of this East African coastal area had had some contacts with Indians, Arabs, and Persians for more than three thousand years, such encounters remained superficial, limited to the inhabitants of the coast. Except for the present-day Moorish architecture of Kenya, foreign contacts have had little influence on the natives. When Jomo returned to Kenya in 1946, his plan of subversion was good and he was the right man to realize it, but the people did not follow him because they were still untouched by modern life.

When Jomo's campaign of rebellion began, the problems facing the British appeared almost insurmountable. British officials were not even sure whether it was Jomo or someone else who led it. The Mau Mau, gangsters of the jungle, were operating in separate groups of twenty to thirty. They did not appear to have any central command. They did things which didn't seem to be rational. The British military intelligence on the spot tried, in terms of western European thinking, to guess what they would do next, but the answers didn't come out right. Jomo seemed always on the march and moving about. He had organized semilegal, overt schools for training his people in what appeared to be almost legal operations. In the classroom, he cautiously refrained from advising them to go out and kill, which would have been dangerous for him. He simply preached the evils of the British government and the need of his people to obtain their complete freedom. His school somewhat resembled New York City's Jefferson School.

Things did not work out so well for Jomo. His fanatical Mau Mau, which he had organized in 1948, soon got out of hand. Their actions turned to open, cruel violence, which is supposed to be step two or three, not step one, in the pattern of subversion according to the Communist manual. Although the Mau Mau swung almost immediately into small units, they used semi-military tactics as they set up roadblocks, raided farms, seized hostages, blew up bridges, stole guns, and tortured their own people.

Things went worse for Jomo when the British sent Evelyn Baring, an extraordinary man, to Kenya as governor. He knew Africa, had served there for many years. He was familiar with the terrain, and he knew the natives better than they knew themselves. He understood what needed to be done, and what was even more important, he knew how to get the British government to do it.

A modest man, Governor Baring gave much of the credit to his military commander when he explained the situation to me. Major General Hinde, now Sir Robert Hinde and retired, also had intimate knowledge of the land and its people; he and his brother owned farms in Kenya, and his hunting trips had taken him to all of its most remote corners. Many of the local British settlers who stood by to defend themselves also knew the country. When they had dinner at home or drinks at their club, they put their guns next to them on the table, ready to shoot if necessary. One settler, a youngster by the name of Francis Erskine, would dye his hair and black his face to lead a band of Kikuyus against the Mau Mau.

The new governor was quick to suspect Jomo as the mastermind of Mau Mau; during his first months of duty, he followed Jomo on all his travels. Since he found that violence flared up at every place Jomo visited, he was soon sure of Jomo's leading role.

Jomo's first appeal was inherited from his grandfather, who had been a witch doctor. Like his ancestor, Jomo knew how to gather native groups in the woods for secret rites, and he was also reputed to have hypnotic eyes. Jomo's appeal was double barreled, almost paradoxically so, for above his traditional appeals with witch doctor's magic, he had the more modern appeal of having been educated in the ways of the West. At the age of ten, a Church of Scotland mission befriended him. Since he had no name, they called him John Stone. He worked as a carpenter and later as a meter reader in the Nairobi waterworks. A British family aided him with books and advice. His training in modern ways was soon so advanced that he could edit a newspaper for the Kikuyus' Central Association. In 1931, he began his studies in London, which lasted for fifteen years and were interrupted only by trips to Moscow. It was at this time that he took up the name Jomo Burning Sphere Kenyatta. He studied Communism in the freedom of England, which years ago also gave Lenin refuge, and, like Lenin, he abused it for the destruction of those who had befriended him.

In Kenya, the British followed Jomo's steps. Whenever he appeared in a forest gathering, his hypnotic personality and his brilliant oratory attracted crowds of two or three thousand. Oaths were given, and after Kenyatta's visit, it was always observed that the people were sullen and seemingly fearful. They were taking such oaths as: "If I am instructed to kill a white and do not do it, then my oath will come and kill me. If I am of assistance to a European in his operations against a fellow Mau Mau, then this oath will kill me." And after Jomo's visit to a locality, there appeared ominous warnings, such as a strangled cat hung at the entrance of the hut of a tribesman who had refused to take the oath; then a crime would follow, perhaps the hideous murder of the tribesman or the disemboweling of his entire family. This, in turn, would be followed by other sinister deeds against tribesmen and British.

Jomo was too clever to be caught red handed, but the circumstances pointed clearly to him. Baring presented the facts to British authorities in London and was given permission to take prompt steps before it was too late. British troops were flown to Kenya in secret to be ready if and when the situation got out of hand. Then, in lightning raids, 107 leaders of the Mau Mau were arrested. Only a half-dozen of the top leaders escaped to the jungle, where they were picked up much later, along with hundreds of second-level leaders from towns and various jungle areas. To destroy the leadership was tantamount to destroying the whole movement. That the British employed this strategy annoyed the Communists to no end, for it is their own favorite technique.

Next, the British grouped the Kikuyus into guarded villages, with little holdings of a half-acre each scattered in clearings. In these villages, the Kikuyus were safe; they didn't have to obey the threats of the Mau Mau, and they could be controlled, while those outside could be identified as enemies. The remaining Mau Mau were bombed by British aircraft, attacked by land, and starved out. Finally, when the time was ripe, an amnesty was offered. "Come in, come out of the woods, be fed—you'll be forgiven." Several hundred, including some leaders, responded to the appeal and gave themselves up. Jomo's movement looked like a lost cause for them.

At this stage of the game, every little Mau Mau leader had

come to call himself a general—General China, General Russia, General Tanganyika, General This, General That. General China led the way into surrender. He turned over to the British information on the workings of the jungle post-office system, and told them how Mau Mau messages were hid in the crotch of a tree or in a hole in a log. The British began to drop their own messages in these new post offices to tell the Mau Mau of the hopelessness of their position, offering them amnesty if they surrendered promptly. The appeal worked. While previously only common followers, sent into town for raids by their leaders, who themselves stayed in the security of the woods, had been captured, the workers now began to demand that their leaders come out too. This led to the capture of more leaders; others surrendered. The movement of the Mau Mau was on its way to complete disintegration. From the Mau Mau point of view, the worst of all happened when Jomo lost control of his own people. The British had "beaten him to the punch."

The Mau Mau uprising has followed the course of many other African emotional outbursts of the past. Like the Zulus, who in their day had marched across the country, killing everything, animate and inanimate, until in the end they became one of the most docile tribes of Africa, the Mau Mau had flared up and consumed themselves quickly. As the well-known British anthropologist L. S. B. Leakey has found, African flare-ups have a common pattern: they burn intensely for a short time, like sticks and grass, but if controlled, they burn out rapidly. The British handled and aided this process in Kenya with clever efficiency.

And what next? When I passed through Kenya and was served by the dressed but barefooted waiters in the New Stanley Hotel, I found it hard to believe that their revolt was all over. The British don't believe it's all over, either. They have simply put down violence with violence and are now proceeding with their long-range plans for the gradual evolution of the local population through education, economic improvement, and advancement of political conscience.

A new native leader named Tom Mboya, as skillful and subtle as Jomo Kenyatta, is now coming to the forefront of Kenya leadership. He is very different from Jomo. Determined to obtain independence and sovereignty for his people through legal methods, along the pattern of Kwame Nkrumah of Ghana, he has already made some political progress in the last election. The 6,000,000 Africans were allowed to elect eight black members for the National Legislative Council. The 42,000 whites of Kenya are represented by fourteen members, while the 159,000 Indians, the ever busy craftsmen and businessmen of the area, have six representatives and the miscellaneous Arabs, who number approximately 50,000, one representative.

Only thirty years old, Mboya may well achieve, with his methods of persuasion and lawfulness, what Jomo failed to achieve with his methods of violence. That Mboya is gaining recognition of a sort is borne out by the fact that he was asked to be chairman of the first All Africa Peoples' Conference held at Accra, Ghana, in late 1958. His intemperate insult of "Scram from Africa," shouted at the non-black rulers of Africa, and his defense of Jomo Kenyatta were highlighted with the same organized cheers that were given to greetings from Khrushchev. "We will welcome the day," said one highly placed Briton to me, "when the whites, the blacks, and the browns can work together in complete economic, social, and political equality. After all, we Englishmen have always been known for our tolerance, but equality isn't something which you get by shooting somebody or claiming you are equal; it's something which must be worked for."

As I see it, the Africans have been at work for this, and they still are. What they must do now is to think about this goal and find ways to arrive at it. Here, as elsewhere in backward areas, education is the key to real social and economic evolution. Americans can only wait—and hope—for the success of this evolution, but we surely must not oppose British colonial power with antagonistic prejudices. In fact, the British deserve our sympathy when they squelch Moscow-led native leaders of revolution and when they assist the natives in their gradual progress.

6 Sudan: Promise of Progress

If American foreign policy were concerned only with military security, as some maintain, the Sudan would hardly pose a problem of importance to this country. Rather than of military or even political interest at the present time, the Sudan's problems, which might well turn into serious political dilemmas of deep concern to us later, are of an economic nature.

Sudan's economic problems have been brought about by its recent emergence as an independent nation. They stem from its backwardness, as well as from its sudden loss of colonial rule, which, clichés to the contrary notwithstanding, was not always bad for the colonies; there are at least as many brands of colonialism as there are shades of color in a rainbow. In fact, Sudan's problems arose only when it won its independence. This event took place in 1952 when its people, multilingual, multiracial, and more than 80 per cent illiterate, were asked to vote on a simple question: "Do you want the Sudan to be tied to Egypt or to Great Britain or to nobody at all?" The final outcome indicated that the majority chose the third alternative, complete independence in a "do-it-yourself" way, for their nation.

After this vote was taken, the real work began. In the first place, a poor people has to be led on the road to economic health. Success depends mainly on what the new leaders do with the waters of the Blue Nile and the White Nile, which join at Khartoum, flow northwards through Egypt to the Mediterranean, and are the very life line of the country. What is also needed to bring success to Sudan is a new system of leadership—political, administrative, economic. The Sudan has set to work on all these issues, a big job that we cannot understand without looking back at what has made Sudan the nation that it is today.

The Sudan, with more than a million square miles of territory, is one-fourth the size of all Europe. It stretches from the southern border of the temperate zone to three degrees north of the equator, a length of more than thirteen hundred miles, ranging from arid deserts to flatland prairies to damp tropical forests. Roughly, the north is Arab, Islamic in faith, civilized, worldly, while the south is Negroid, pagan, primitive, isolated. The various peoples that make up the interior include Arab camelkeepers in the deserts, racially mixed farmers on the Nile borders, and tall, Negroid, cattle-raising tribesmen in the south.

The prevalent mixture of Arab and Negro blood stems from the Islamic institution of slavery, which was brought to the Sudan in the seventh century by all-conquering Arabs who raided the south to bring home native slaves and concubines (at that time, a wealthy Arab was allowed as many concubines as he could afford). This practice eventually brought about not only a mixture of bloods but also a distrust of the north which remains today and shows itself in spoken and unspoken animosity between southern and northern Sudanese.

The long and varied history of the Sudan does not bear out those clichés which condemn the white man and the white man's civilization. True, seven thousand years ago, Sudanese made clay pots resembling baskets which, in some areas untouched by the white man, are still produced in excellent quality today. But the really great advances of this fine people have been made possible only by the white man's civilization, mostly under the influence of British colonizers during the last fifty years.

Native tribal rule and primitive society had been destroyed by 1820, when Mehemet Ali, who had established himself as ruler of Egypt under the Ottoman sultan, sent his armies to take over the Sudan. The connection, by the way of Egypt, with Turkey endured until the British ended it at the beginning of World War I. The Turks left the people of the Sudan to their own chaotic administrative devices from 1820 until 1881, when a bloody revolution took place under a religious fanatic, Mahommed Ahmed, the son of a boat-builder from Dongola, who claimed to be the Mahdi, or leader, of Islam. His disciples were the howling dervishes and the whirling dervishes, both sects living faithfully up to their names. By 1884, this cruel zealot and his followers had taxed, butchered, starved, tortured, and reduced the Sudanese population from 8,500,000 to less than 2,000,000, with villages burned, cattle destroyed, and fig trees chopped down. It was about this time that the British, who had come to Egypt in defense of their nationals, began to take an active hand in the affairs of the Sudan, which had been nominally under the control of Egypt. At first, the British recommended to the khedive of Egypt that the Sudan be completely abandoned by them. Only after considerable fumbling in London, and after the annihilation of an entire Egyptian army under the command of the British Colonel Hicks, was it decided to bring order to the Sudan. Under strong British guidance during the past fifty years, the Sudanese have made great progress in administration of government, economic matters, and the training of Sudanese leaders.

The leading Sudanese who fought British rule in our times until his nation had won independence was Abdullah Khalil. Over seventy years of age, he was prime minister and unifying force of his country and was, in a way, the equivalent of Chancellor Konrad Adenauer in present-day West Germany. Though ousted from office by the military junta of November 17, 1958, he remains one of the Sudan's influential and extraordinary personalities. Foxy, and as profoundly honest as Adenauer, he has unwavering principles. One of his supporters criticized him for a statement he made at a meeting of the Parliament, provoking opposition. "Was it true what I stated or wasn't it?" Khalil asked him, and continued: "It was true; therefore I am glad I said it."

When he granted me an exclusive interview (we were sipping excellent fruit juice, as is the general and continuous custom in his country, where the average temperature simmers around eighty degrees and the body needs great amounts of fluids, alcohol in any form being forbidden), I was impressed by his friendship for Great Britain, which he had fought since 1925. "We are with the West, not the East," he assured me. "We want relations with those who can help us—the Americans and the British. We don't want to be stuck with those who are less advanced than we are. We in the Sudan may not be highly civilized, but we have our quiet qualities. We are conservatives by nature, experience, and religion. We build on the old. We don't destroy the old to get some untried new thing. My home is an example," he proudly pointed out, "I live in the area where my father lived and where I was raised. First my floor was packed dirt; then, as my income and station improved, I made it concrete. Now I put red tile on top. I've never been tied to the material things of life. I don't even have a bedroom in my house. I sleep on the porch or where-ever it happens to be coolest. I could sleep right out there under Allah's beautiful sky," said he, sweeping his arm to the great out-doors beyond the window.

Although Khalil is now out of office, his homely philosophy of moderation is likely to continue to guide the policies of the Sudan. His son-in-law, General Ahmed Abdel Wahab, is the Number 2 man in the new government. The seizure of control by Sudanese Army Commander Ibrahim Abboud was accomplished without either bloodshed or arrests, and the new government has ex-pressed its intentions to adhere to the Sudan's international obli-gations.

When I visited the Sudan in 1957, it was apparent that some-thing had to give, for the newly created republic had not yet learned to govern itself, was not ready for free-wheeling democ-racy. For example, the elected and appointed heads of govern-ment did not respect and use their British-trained Sudanese civil servants, and the legislative bodies were more inclined to argue and haggle than to put through essential measures for the eco-nomic betterment of the people. The differing racial, religious, social, economic, and political factions were pulling in different directions and getting nowhere. The military junta, if wise, may succeed in getting essential actions, such as the building of a road from Khartoum to Wad Medani. At the same time, it can train and educate the Sudanese in the ways and means of political, social and economic evolution.

Despite economic advances, the Sudanese are still a very poor people; the plight of the northern farmers, who grub a living from the soil along the Nile, is even worse than that of the southern Sudanese, who live by and with cattle. The over-all number of animals in the Sudan in 1952 included 1,100,000 camels, mostly in the north and cared for by Arabs; 3,200,000 head of cattle, mostly in the south, owned and cared for by the Nilotic tribes; 4,800,000 sheep; and 4,000,000 goats. The lives of the cattle growers, the Baggara, are so closely related to their cattle that a tribesman of the Nuer tribe, for instance, is usually identified in society by his cow. He might be known as Mr. Black and White Spot, though the "Mister" part is usually dropped.

Sudan's exports include foodstuffs and some agricultural and animal products. Imports consist mostly of tea, sugar, coffee, and tobacco. A favorable balance of trade prevails, but this means little in view of the fact that there is extremely little foreign trade altogether. In 1951, the biggest export, cotton, was valued at £45,500,000 Egyptian, while the most valuable import was piece goods worth £10,000,000 Egyptian.

The solution to Sudan's water problem can bring about a healthy economic evolution. The Nile means life to Egypt and opportunity for the Sudan. Significantly, one of the first publications of the new government concerned Sudan's irrigation, with plans for many dams and a giant drainage canal far to the south, where wet swamplands and dried areas of flowing grass alternate. If these blueprinted developments, controlling the headwaters of the Nile, come to pass, the Egyptian government will find itself directly concerned, for even a bucket of water taken out of the Nile in the Sudan could result in the death of a family along the Egyptian Nile, where more than 80 per cent of the population ekes out a living from the low, as well as the high, waters of the Nile. The mouth of the Nile River where it flows into the Mediterranean is, during the the dry season, dammed with mud to keep sea water from coming back into Egypt. Every drop of the Nile's water is being used for a second crop along the banks of this, the only fertile land of all Egypt.

Irrigation projects are likely to affect the entire social, economic, moral, and political thinking of the Sudan. One such project is the proposed Jonglei Canal, which would cut 130 miles through swampland from Jonglei, on the White Nile, to Malakal, around the bend of the same river. It would run through areas where the Nuer and other Nilotic tribes live by and with their cattle. If this land is drained, hundreds of thousands of acres of soil will be available to agriculture. According to estimates, the realization of this and additional developments would make available fertile soil sufficient to feed an additional twenty-two million persons instead of the three or four million persons who now depend upon unpredictable, irregular animal husbandry in land alternately flooded and parched.

"Control the waters of the Nile in the Sudan and you control Egypt." This is still as true today as it was a hundred years ago. But if dams and irrigation projects are built in the Sudan, what immigrants will be allowed to settle and to cultivate the additional lands? Will they come from central Africa or will the Egyptians be permitted to send their overflowing population into these lands? Is it better to hold the waters of the Nile far to the south rather than to attempt to hold the waters behind a giant dam known as the Higher Aswan? The Higher Aswan Dam, if built, would hold water for a distance of 400 miles, 130 miles of which would be in the Sudan and 270 miles in Egypt. There is much to be said for the storage of the waters of the Nile far south in the Sudan, and it can be assumed that in the coming debates, these points will be brought out forcefully by the Sudanese.

U.S. Ambassador Lowell C. Pinkerton is watching the development of the Sudan-Egyptian water problem: "There are many complications and involvements," he explained to me, "but, at the risk of oversimplification, it boils down to just one fact: the Nile water available for use supplies Egypt with forty-eight billion cubic meters of water a year. The Sudanese get four billion cubic meters. During the flood season, an additional thirty-two billion cubic meters of water flow into the Mediterranean. This extra water is what the argument is all about. The Agreement of 1929, between the British and the Egyptians, assured the Egyptians that no additional projects would be undertaken in the

Sudan which might injure the water interests of Egypt. Of course, the present Sudanese government was not part of this agreement and therefore might ignore it. However, they have fully respected it up to now. The disputed question is, who will get the thirty-two billion cubic meters of water if and when provision is made for its storage and use? The Sudanese would like to get at least a fifty-fifty arrangement, which would give them sixteen billion cubic meters, while Egypt could have an additional sixteen billion for itself. But the Egyptians have other ideas; they would prefer a distribution keyed to population numbers, which would give them two-thirds of the additional water, while one-third would go to the Sudanese."

These figures were confirmed by Sudanese Deputy Permanent Under-Secretary Minister of Affairs Sayed Babikir el Deeb. He indicated that the Sudanese would not debate forever but would go ahead with some of their water-project plans. However, he was confident that peaceful arrangements could be worked out with the Egyptian government as soon as the excitement quieted down.

The typical Sudanese family, though clean and well dressed after the day's work is done, is still very poor. According to estimates, the head of a family earns about £15 Egyptian (about $45) a month. His children work at odd jobs, while his wife may sell vegetables or perform other services to bring in additional money until the total family income comes close to $65 a month.

But progress is visible. In what was the slum of Khartoum, a community development has been organized in which thirty thousand of the city's seventy thousand inhabitants now live. The city gives to the head of the family 200 square meters, roughly 167 square yards, of free land on which he can build his own house. For those of larger income, 400 square meters are given, and this grant is increased up to 1,600 square meters for the highest income group. Three models of houses are shown for the lowest brackets; it is up to the individual which of the three he will choose. In the second income group, a man selects his own type of house but must receive city approval of it, while in the third and highest group, everybody may build as he wants unless the city objects to it.

The most interesting developments are those in the poorest income brackets. I watched some men building their own houses by piling up layer on layer of clay, which is obtained right in the front or back yard. If hired men do the job, a mud house can be built for as little as the Sudanese equivalent of $400. Inside, on the clay floor, which is pounded down after having been wet, there are normally four rooms: one for cooking, one for toilet facilities, and two for living and sleeping purposes. The roof is held on top of the walls by parallel wooden poles which usually stick out on either side. Cow dung has been used extensively as a building material in Sudan ever since it was discovered, at about the same time as in India, more than a hundred years ago, what an excellent plaster ordinary clay makes when a little straw and fermented cow dung are admixed. Of course this doesn't smell too pleasant until the first rain comes. After that, it is said, there is practically no odor. The cementing qualities of the mixture are not only cheap but also excellent.

In this city development, each of the eight blocks has a giant, square, open area where the people gather, where the dogs run around, and where the goats cavort. There is a grain market in the area, built by the city, and some meat stalls. On this lowest income level, real-estate development seems very low living indeed to an American, but to people who formerly were living in "tin cans" or shacks built of sticks and stones, this is organized community living and a better life.

Next to dams and irrigation, the future of Sudan and its cities depends on the success of new agricultural experiments on the pattern of the Gazira experiment, a test case already successfully realized. Since everybody in Sudan talked about it, I was eager to visit it and said so to the Acting Chief of Protocol, Sayed Ahmed Hassan Mattar. "This," he told me quickly, "can be arranged. When do you want to go—tomorrow?" "Why yes," I said, and expected a short run the hundred miles down to the Gazira and back without expenditure of much energy or time. "Very good," said this first-class arranger, "the car should pick you up at five o'clock in the morning and you will be there in time to talk with the governor at nine o'clock. You will be able to see, in practically no time, the farm projects and the cotton ginning mills."

The ride turned out to be something of a surprise. At five in the morning, my driver picked me up at the hotel in a new red Ford station wagon, and away we went on the hard-topped road toward the outskirts of town. But after passing the airport near the city limits, the road disappeared. "A short detour," I thought (there wasn't any point in my talking to my driver because neither of us understood the other), "undoubtedly they're fixing the road." An hour later, literally flying across trackless desert and having skidded, slipped, and had my backbone jolted by the roughest terrain I've ever crossed, not excluding those in a jeep during the war, I felt that I could take no more. But it lasted for four more hours. We went through mud villages, pushed cows out of the way, honked our way through the herds of goats, and gave that Ford car a going-over that no "torture field" at the Ford plant could duplicate. If Ford wants a testimonial on the durability of its cars, I'll give it free!

At exactly nine o'clock, we arrived at the headquarters, or rather the home, of the acting governor of the Gazira. He met me, smiling, at his door. He claims to be only an inch over six feet, but I think he forgot to measure a few inches of his height; he must be close to seven feet, like many of the slim, giant tribesmen of the far south from which his mother came. His father was an Arab from the North. To hear him talk, you would think you were speaking to a very, very British gentleman in khaki shorts, long khaki safari jacket, and military helmet in the British tradition. He had arranged a light breakfast for me, which I promptly devoured. Then we rode together to the headquarters of the Gazira, in the center of the town of Wad Medani. "You'll excuse me," he said, "while I inspect the guards." He walked over to the honor guard, which consisted of about fifty men of different sizes and heights, all dressed in the uniform of the Gazira police department. One of them blew on his horn, and immediately every-body saluted.

From then on, the Governor was busy with details of work at his desk. These men who are taking over a nation have got a twenty-four-hour day's work to do every day of the week. But the thirty-one thousand persons living on the farms and laboring desperately hard are apparently happy. Before, they had, with even harder work, produced only about seventy-five cents an acre; the government still pays tenants for their lands at this rate. Half of all the land, however, belongs to the government, which gives each tenant forty acres of land to cultivate on his own with his family or hired hands. His land is irrigated by a great water project, drawing water to this delta area from the Blue Nile, an impressive, all-gravity-flow canal system. Each forty-acre plot is divided into four equal sections, with two sections planted in cotton, while one ten-acre plot can be used by the farmer for growing grain and other foods for his own use or to sell. The fourth plot of ten acres must remain fallow and is rotated by government order. All cotton picked, and that's the money crop, is gathered and turned over to the central administration for ginning and marketing. The tenant farmer gets his share of the over-all earnings, which amount to 40 per cent of the profits for the tenants, 40 per cent for the government, and 20 per cent for the administration.

The ginning mill I visited had about 120 ginning machines operating full blast on a round-the-clock basis. The Negro women, a few men, and some children, busy at those machines work a twelve-hour day for a compensation of four shillings, fifty cents, a day. As I learned, a great number of Mohammedans from the western coast, passing through on their way to Mecca, remain or return to work here. The whole operation in this ginning mill would not satisfy American union standards, but different standards are required when a people tries to pull itself up from nothing. Since the people working in this first phase of industrial revolution are so much better off than they were before, there are no complaints. However, the Communists are already suggesting that the government is working them too hard. The government is anxious to have them work hard, indeed, for two reasons: first, for their own gain and second, for the profit of the government which will channel these earnings into other new project developments for the people. Almost 50 per cent of the revenue of the Sudanese government comes from this one modernly operated cotton farm. When some of the other ten million Sudanese approach the productivity of the thirty-one thousand workers of Gazira, many of the fiscal problems of the Sudan will be solved.

"At any rate," Sayed el Deeb told me, "the Sudanese are pleased with their freedom and will resent any attempts at interference by Egypt, by Britain, or by any other outside government."

"What about the drainage canal of the White Nile?" I asked him. "If that's completed and goes through, I understand that it is estimated that the agricultural land made available could feed as many as twenty-two million persons. Where would they come from? Where would the farmers come from for this vast farming project? Would the Egyptian farmers be allowed to migrate?"

"Oh no! Not right now!" said el Deeb. "There are too many political differences of opinion at this moment for anything so far-reaching as that to be worked out."

When I asked him what he considered his most urgent needs right now, he mentioned outside capital, to pay for the water developments, but he followed this immediately by pointing to the need for foreign advisors to substitute for the British, from civil service to technicians, engineers, and teachers. How useful the British had been was further borne out by the brilliant Deputy Permanent Under-Secretary Minister of the Interior, Sayed Dawood Abdel Latif: "The British did a fine job of training a civil service," he admitted, "but in the long run, the Sudanese will make out better governing themselves. The new government, once it strikes its stride, will key its procedures and plans to the psychology of the Sudanese people. The Sudanese, with their strong reliance upon the Mohammedan religion, its customs, and its practices, always objected to having to adjust to foreign thinking and foreign ways, even when these foreign ways were good ways. The British made a tremendous fuss over details, while the Sudanese think mostly in terms of the principle of things."

This, of course, opens an educational job for the Sudanese, as Mohamed A. Yagi explained. "Freedom of choice in education is very important to a new nation such as ours," said Dr. Yagi. "When the British controlled our administration, the tendency was for a local Sudanese, such as me, to be sponsored by a local British administrator and sent to a British university. If a Sudanese, by chance, went to some other country for his education, he just did not seem to fit into the pattern upon his return. I was unemployed two years after receiving my doctorate at the Sorbonne. Now we are free to send our students to different countries for different specialties. You, Dr. Howley, have been talking with Mr. Hosni, who has just received his doctorate in philosophy from New York University. We have other students who may come to the United States to study medicine, while some will go to France to study art, and others may go to England to study international law. For election procedures we have found the study of the systems of India most useful to us. This freedom to choose the world's best schools helps our educational and our cultural development a great deal."

The Sudanese need foreign teachers badly. At the time of the British termination of leadership in 1952, approximately the following number of trained Sudanese had been occupying important positions in the Ministry of Health: 106 doctors, 445 medical assistants, 648 midwives, 181 nurses, 20 dispensers, 14 assistant radiographers, 38 public health officers, and 119 sanitary overseers. Gordon College, which was established at the turn of the century, has grown to a fully recognized college as part of the University College of Khartoum. The Kitchener School of Medicine, with its faculty of medicine, was also incorporated into that university on September 1, 1951. A girl's school, a rare thing in an Arab-controlled country, was founded in 1907.

The British carried out a deliberately planned policy of their own abdication from control of Sudanese affairs. According to their plans, the majority of professional and civil service jobs were to be in Sudanese hands by 1962, and at the time of the British departure, they were very close to their schedule of native training. Those who advocate more rapid advances in the turning of Sudanese affairs over to the Sudanese criticize the British for not having set up an even speedier timetable, but it still remains to be seen whether the new leadership, having assumed full responsibility, will not have sacrificed in the process the gradual completion of the British plans.

In economics, the Sudanese problem is simple: "Now that we're independent, who can help us most?" This question involves not only the Sudanese themselves but also Nasser, their other Arab neighbors, and the Soviets, who are constantly trying to extend their present sphere of influence. "We Sudanese are anti-Communist, you Americans are anti-Communist, and you also stand for other things which we uphold. These are points of view that we have in common," the Prime Minister assured me. "But the Communists are trying to cause trouble, particularly among our youth. They work through a few Sudanese, but these Sudanese are bought; they don't really represent the people."

The U.S. Ambassador agrees with this view. "The Communists," he told me, "are very active here, but they won only one seat in the last election, despite their complete freedom during the campaign, and their following is far less than one per cent. Yet, as you know, Communists love to fish in troubled waters. They are very busy in attempting to get control of trade-unions. But they present no danger yet."

As one Sudanese minister told me, "The Communists are not interested in helping us to solve our problems. They are only interested in getting control of leadership." In the Russian Embassy at Khartoum, there are eighty-two Russians whose working aims, I might add, are rather obscure, while the Sudanese Embassy in Moscow consists of only two men. Occasionally, a Russian "diplomat" is caught directing activities against the Sudanese government, but most often the Soviets work through elaborately printed propaganda literature produced in Beirut, Lebanon, and shipped into Sudan. The misnamed "neutral" agencies of India or local bought-off Sudanese are other transmission belts they prefer.

"We're a new nation," said one minister. "We don't know quite how to handle this clever propaganda, designed to discredit our government. We need your help. I hope that you will continue to support your United States Information Service. Our youth have nothing to read. Consequently, they read the Soviet propaganda which is flooding the country. But your information service is very effective, and they will just as readily read American material about the other side of the story." My quick visit to the USIA office gave me the same impression. It does effective work and offers attractive, if not persuasive, material. Our money, spent to explain the facts of life, as we see it, to the Sudanese, will, in the long run, be more than repaid.

As a member of the Sudanese government pointed out to me, the Islamic faith of the Sudanese is completely contradictory to Communism. Islam admonishes its followers: "Live right and work right and you will be rewarded after death." The Communists say: "Live right and work right and you will get great rewards in this life." The older people recognize the limitations of what we can attain, but youth sees only its own wants and falls for the phony prophets of abundance. The Communists exploit this by inviting hundreds of young Sudanese, all expenses paid, to Moscow—as "guests of private, non-governmental youth groups."

Conflicts between Sudan and other nations are bound to arise. It must be assumed that the present irrigation plans of the government of Sudan will meet with vigorous and even violent opposition from Egypt. Under United Nations agreements, the right of conquest no longer has validity. Can the Egyptians still claim a right to waters which have not yet reached the Egyptian border when Sudan is an independent country? And should America help the Sudanese to prosperity and wealth or force them to share their water assets with the fellows down the stream?

All the while, the new Sudanese leaders will remain preoccupied with their domestic problems: how to convert people from animal husbandry to dirt farming; how to bring about essential centralized control of economic evolution in a backward area when the people oppose all administration and prefer complete decentralization. If you build a hydro-electric power plant or a dam, it brings power into small shops and electricity into the homes; in short, it ushers in a new civilization of electronics. What happens to a people who have been trained for centuries in austerity when they find themselves with an abundance of food and a minimum of back-breaking labor? How does one plan for a quick industrial revolution where backward people jump from villages to towns? What should be the guiding principle concerning immigration of neighboring peoples into newly made fertile lands? How do you adjust a primitive people, accustomed to isolation, to the varied problems of contact with highly civilized countries? Should the Sudanese government attempt to solve all of its problems alone, under a mantle of extreme nationalism, or should it attempt to solve these joint economic, political, and social problems with its neighbors—Egypt, the Belgian Congo, Uganda, Kenya, French Equatorial Africa, Ethiopia? Perhaps jointly through the Arab League? Can this new nation spring full grown into the arms of world citizenship by way of a distorted notion of the United Nations organization? And what must we do about it, if anything?

The lesson which the Sudanese are already learning is a lesson that should be learned by more advanced Western democracies. It is the simple fact that a government may plan and direct beneficial developments and progressive changes for its people, but the developments and changes themselves must be worked out and sweated out by the people. Whether with heavy taxations, as in the United States, or with a twelve-hour, fifty-cent day, as in the Gazira, it is the people who pay for anything they get. The Sudanese government seems to understand this and therefore does not ask us for much.

If the goal of our foreign policy is to help people who are less fortunate and less advanced than we are to help themselves, the Sudan, with its poor people, its sensible attitude toward God and man, its confident, hard-working government, deserves both our attention and our help. How long it will take the Sudanese to achieve economic health and educational fitness and how much longer it will be before Sudan can even think of democratic organization are not for us to decide.

7 Egypt: Dreams on the Nile

The first Egyptian I saw from my hotel-room balcony was a fisherwoman. She sat with her son in one of the many boats that drift lazily on the Nile with the current or sail softly upstream with the wind. The day before, and all the years before, even when her country had been invaded and her city bombed, she and her sons had sailed and drifted, dragging their long net in exactly the same fashion. Their reward for this day's labor was at best two fish, about one pound each. In the market they would be worth a shilling, or fifteen cents, but they would not go to market; she and her family would eat them, probably as their only food for the day. Her thinking centered around the next day's bread rather than around Nasser's dreams and schemes.

During my stay in Egypt, I myself took to the Nile. Up the river, with its old and new irrigation dams and drainage canals, I met the fellahin, the Egyptian farmers. They work the deep-blue soil with their thousand-year-old wooden plow, which is usually pulled by two oxen. The fellah and his five-pound hoe, the *fass,* has been keeping Egypt alive for more than five thousand years. This farmer, with his hoe, like the fisherwoman in her boat, both depend equally upon the Nile, and today, as in the past, Egypt's hopes depend on them.

The Nile Valley supplies the only fertile soil in the wasteland of sand which is Egypt; 85 per cent of her people are engaged in cultivating this 4 per cent of the soil. The average amount available with present intensive irrigation is less than three acres per farm family or, on a national basis, including the city population, less than one-third of an acre per capita.

The Egyptians have seen rulers come and go. They were conquered by the Persians in 525 B.C., were ruled by the Ptolemies for almost three centuries, then by the Romans, followed by Arabs, Turks, British, French, and a multitude of other nations in continuous sequence. All these foreign rulers had one thing in common: they lived in the cities, ruled from their palaces, and cared little whether the fellahin lived or died, so long as they supplied them with food.

The greatness of Egypt, revealed in astronomy, mathematics, art, philosophy, and religion, was not of the Nile farmer's making. He laboriously hoed the rich ground when the annual floods of the Nile had receded. He also pushed giant blocks of stone on crude rollers and often felt the blood-letting slash of the hippopotamus whip so that the Egyptian rulers could lie in security beneath their pyramids after death. If the fellahin were docile and not at all eager to defend Cleopatra and her lover, Marc Antony, against the Roman legions or to fight for and against anyone else, it's hard to blame them, and they have not changed little since those times.

Food, or rather the lack of it, has always been a problem in Egypt, and when the annual floods on the Nile fail to come, as has been the case many times, there is widespread want and starvation. That Egypt has suffered from the lack of food, as well as from other pertinent factors, is reflected in the drastic decline of the Egyptian population since the end of Roman rule. The population fell from 7,000,000 during Roman days to 2,500,000 about the turn of the nineteenth century. The Islamic faith, the predominant religion of Egypt, with its stress on predestination, charity by almsgiving, and freedom from racial intolerance, may not favor economic fermentation.

Mehemet Ali, during the nineteenth century, claimed that he promoted Egyptian industry, whether they liked it or not, in order to train his people in manufacturing. His mission, he said, was to advance his people rather than to make a profit. He aimed to educate the Egyptians in the ways of the West and in the techniques of running armies and governments by means of a utilitarian approach. His British successors contributed much to

Egypt's progress, but as a British writer said: "It just goes to prove that even efficiency and uplifting are poor substitutes for self-rule." Or as an Egyptian government official said to me: "We'd rather be free to run our own affairs, even though we make mistakes, than live in an economic paradise under foreign domination."

The present government of Egypt, the first native government, is dedicated to the welfare of its people and based on the mass allegiance of these people. Yet the leaders are still groping for the best way of rebuilding and rejuvenating their once great nation. Should they perhaps follow Bismarck, who with military victories proved Germany's greatness to the German people? Battles are normally won by hard men rather than gentle, kind, patient people; the victorious bayonet is driven and the killing bullet directed with a snarl, not a friendly smile. Therefore, the Egyptian way to start the complicated growth of the nation's economic, social, and political life does not seem to be the way of the sword, since the average fellah is not a modern fighter. The only people the Egyptians could logically fight would be the Israelis, who are tough opponents indeed, as they have proved by two major victories in the last ten years.

The real future of Egypt is the Nile, as the Egyptian government officials agree. However, their national emotions often tend to negate this rational admission. Whether it's General Naguib, who didn't do enough, or Colonel Nasser, who tries too much, Egypt sometimes seems to resemble the rider of a beautiful white horse whom I watched in Cairo's traffic. The rider was pulling the checkrein while spurring his Arab mount. Pulling the checkrein stops a horse, while spurring him in the flanks makes him go forward. Since the horse was unable to do both at once, he settled for spinning, bucking, and snorting while the rider told passing truck drivers and pedestrians what he thought of them as well as of his horse.

Egypt's improvements of its way of life with agricultural and industrial progress are hampered by its hostile inclinations toward and preparations against Israel, its eleven-year-old neighbor. Seizing the Suez Canal and defending Egypt against the

Israelis, French, and British cost Egypt more than it would have cost to build the High Aswan Dam. Raising the more than forty-nine sunken ships and clearing out the fallen bridges, which turned the Suez Canal into a watery junkyard—a job well done by General Wheeler and his German salvage crews—alone cost more than fifty million dollars.

But then, as was impressed on me by each Cairo talk, the actions of Egypt cannot be judged in terms of the logic of the West. The Egyptians are as irrational at times as the Orientals, whom they copy. Why this most ancient of civilizations should copy anybody else is hard to understand, but again and again, the main argument offered me was, "After all, we are Orientals." Yet, in fact, the only thing Oriental about these great cities of Alexandria and Cairo that I found were the so-called Oriental dancers in night clubs. When I was a boy and the circus came to town, they were called hootchy-kootchy dancers or Egyptians. The Orient had never known them.

During my visit to Egypt in 1957, my talks with many government administrators, as well as ordinary Egyptian citizens, rounded out the picture of Egypt's present and coming aspirations. Where does Egypt stand today in the power line-up? The first question concerns the Arab League, of which Egypt is the leading member.

"The League of Arab States," said Abdel Khalek Hassouna, secretary-general of the Arab League, a pleasant, persuasive man educated at Cambridge, from which his son was also graduated last year, "is based on the United Nations Charter, which encourages regional groupings. There is no grouping in the world to compare to the common interests of the Arab States. We have common interests of race, culture, customs, traditions, and religions—even the lands which we have occupied for centuries have somewhat similar characteristics. They run from the Middle East across North Africa to the Atlantic. At present, there are eleven members of the League: Libya, Egypt, Sudan, Yemen, Saudi Arabia, Jordan, Lebanon, Iraq, Syria, Tunisia, and Morocco." As it appeared to me, he wanted these states joined by Algeria and a state of Palestine.

Mr. Hassouna has a lovely wife, five children, and a broad knowledge of law and the humanities. One can feel his positive assurance that his aims will be accomplished, whatever other countries may do.

"What is the mission of the League of Arab States?" I asked Mr. Hassouna. "We have more than one mission," he said, "first, liberation of all Arab peoples from foreign political domination until there will be one union of free Arab states from the Red Sea to the Atlantic. The second mission is the unity of all Arab States in the League of Arab States. This means cultural, language, religious, and other unity. It also means social and welfare advances for all. It includes the exchange of students, the sharing of farm knowledge, and the building up of ideal communities. Economic and fiscal unity are included too. A start is made with 25 per cent preferential treatment in tariffs. A single currency is an objective, though not a reality at the present time."

"And its political and military unities?" I asked.

"There is," said the Secretary-General, "no complete political unity at this time because some of our Arab people are still subjected to foreign domination. There is also no military establishment—nothing to correspond in our headquarters to the Security Council at the larger body, the United Nations. Much later, these things might come into being." This was, of course, a short while before Egypt joined the United Arab Republic with Syria and Yemen.

The third mission of the League of Arab States would be the development of all members, Mr. Hassouna explained. Each state would contribute to the common good what it best could, and, he continued, fortunately, each state has something unique, needed by all of the others, to offer. For instance, the Egyptians, pre-eminent in ancient and modern civilization, have an abundance of farmers who are unsurpassed anywhere else in the world in their knowledge of the intensive working of hand-cultivated lands. To name two other examples, the Lebanese are outstanding traders, while Saudi Arabia is rich in oil.

The Arab League is directed by a council which meets bi-annually. It consists of delegations from each of the member states. Each delegation, large or small, has one vote, and important measures, which are presented by the various committees for a vote, are passed only when accepted unanimously. As a permanent home for the League of Arab States, a beautiful new headquarters is now under construction at Cairo.

"May I ask a practical question concerning the operations, Mr. Secretary?" I interrupted. "It is alleged by the French that arms to supply the Algerian rebels are sent in from Egypt, as are also directions for the operation of the revolutionary forces. If this is true, would such forces be directed by the League?" The Secretary denied this with emphasis. True, he said, the League will do everything in its power to bring about liberation short of military operations. It is up to each member state to implement the general objectives in whatever way it sees fit and has competence.

The job which might well prove to be crucial for failure or success of Egypt, as far as its inner health is concerned, is held by Sayed Merai, minister of agrarian reform. An educated, clear-thinking zealot of the better life for the farmers of Egypt, Merai was quick to explain that the life of Egypt depends upon agriculture. "Under the monarchy, the condition of the fellahin was unbearable," he asserted, "while the present government of Egypt has acquired more than a half-million acres of land and made them available to the people. More than 150,000 acres of this amount came from Farouk and his henchmen, who owned vast estates, cared little for the welfare of the tenants, but enjoyed the gay life of the Riviera."

"Did you confiscate their lands or pay them for them?" I asked him. "We gave them a very fair payment," he stated. "They were given thirty-year state bonds paying 3 per cent per year in payment for their lands. Under the old system, the tenant was actually enslaved. His rate of rent was fixed by the big landholder at the end of the year. Sometimes up to 85 per cent of the year's production was taken from him by this arbitrary system. The tenant, on his part, could not leave the land on his own will but could be ejected any time arbitrarily. Now, under the new system, a tenant can be ejected only for non-payment of rent or other legitimate reasons; the maximum rent which he must pay is fixed at seven times the annual tax which the land owner must pay.

"Now no farm owner can have more than two hundred acres for the head of the family and one hundred acres for all of his children; but three hundred acres is all that can be held by any one family. This is generous indeed if you remember that the average family in Egypt has less than three acres of land." It was apparent that he cared deeply about his poor fellow-citizens.

"Actually," he continued, "right now we have a surplus of more than six million farmers living on the intensely cultivated land. We must increase these irrigation projects to make more land available. We must also bear in mind that each year, with our high birth rate, there are approximately 400,000 more mouths to be fed in Egypt. The new water plans, which are based upon the completion of the Aswan and other dams, would add between one and two million additional acres to the present six million acres of cultivated land."

When I asked the Minister of Agrarian Reform what he thought of the Sudanese plan to build dams in the Sudan, his answer was that the new projects would mainly be used to store flood waters behind the dams and that if properly co-ordinated, the storage of water to be used in the Sudan would fit in nicely with the storage plans of Egypt. "We must allow no water to escape to the Mediterranean Sea!" he said. An American, accustomed to seeing the broad Mississippi dump into the Gulf, the Hudson swirl into the Atlantic, and useless water splashed around all over the place, can understand this emphasis on not letting a single drop of water escape into the sea only if he recalls the complete agricultural dependence of these peoples upon the waters of the Nile.

The man in charge of these projects, M. A. Selim, head of the High Aswan Dam Department and a brilliant engineering rough diamond, has taught at the University of California for five years. Being as certain of his engineering facts as he is outspoken in delicate political matters, he resembles many another engineer of many another nationality: I always found it fascinating to see the contrast between the logic with which they treat their engineering field and their irrational temper when a question appeals to their emotions.

"The High Aswan Dam is needed regardless of planned dams in the Upper Nile," Selim assured me. "The High Aswan," he explained, "will hold 130,000,000,000 cubic meters of water. This equals almost three times the present consumption of Egypt, which runs to approximately 50,000,000,000 cubic meters. When completed, the High Aswan Dam will provide water for 4,000,000 more acres of land, and that's what we need. Second, it will store water for the lean years as the first dam with the capacity to carry over water from one year to another. Third, it will provide hydro-electric power for us. We need the power for the pumps to irrigate the land. The old basin method—the one-crop method, a crop based only on the annual flood—is still used in parts of Egypt, but it is not the answer to the future. We also need this electricity for the use of industry, as well as for rural development, in short, the sort of thing which you did in your American Tennessee Valley developments."

"What about the Sudan?" I asked. "How about their storage of water?" Selim pointed out that the Sudan projects would hold back only 3,000,000,000 cubic meters of water, which would enable them to cultivate approximately 4,000,000 acres of land. "It might," he said, "even take them forty years to complete their plans in the Sudan at a cost of up to $720,000,000. This isn't likely to be done tomorrow." As Selim suggested, our use of so much of the Colorado River water will one day cause the same disputes with Mexico that the Sudanese and Egyptians are now ironing out over the Nile.

When I inquired what he thought about the Jonglei Canal across the swamplands in the Sudan, Selim laughed. "You know," he said, "the Sudanese formerly opposed that swamp project, which we developed years ago, because it would force them to social reforms in what could no longer be cattle country. Now they're all for it, but it would probably take twenty-five years to complete and that would not interfere with Egypt's plans. All of these projects, however, should be co-ordinated." At this point, he shifted gears and paid me the compliment of talking "sort of among us Americans," admonishing me: "Why don't you Americans leave us alone? We'll do our own financing. We're the only people apparently who don't demand your money. All we want is your friendship. The cost of the Higher Aswan Dam will finally run about $1,000,000,000, but we'll pay for it—to start with, through the earnings of the Suez Canal."

"You mean," I asked, "that you're going to pay for the Higher Aswan Dam out of Canal earnings and at the same time pay off the original owners of the Canal?"

"We'll build the dam step by step," he snapped. "The first step will be $150,000,000 in cost and run over five years. We can do it."

Selim, who was speaking as a friend of the United States as well as a patriot of Egypt, insisted, as do all the Egyptian newspapers, that the American press lies about Egypt in order to please friends of the state of Israel. At that time, the Egyptian papers still pointed to the refusal of the American government to allow Egypt to buy arms in the United States, to acquire medicine in the United States after the "aggression" and to get surplus wheat, which was subsequently given by the Russians. The Egyptian press has attacked the United States with greater vigor than either France or Great Britain with the claim that we are endeavoring to take the imperialistic place which the French and the British held in the Arab countries until yesterday.

Factually, the U.S. and Britain withdrew their offers of financial aid in 1956 when Nasser made a deal for guns with Czechoslovakia. Subsequently, Khrushchev, on October 23, 1958, offered Egypt a credit of $100,000,000 to help build the dam.

It was this painful problem which I discussed with Mohamed Abdel Kader Hatem, director-general of informational administration and a sensible, quiet, competent professional in the field of public relations, in which I'm not exactly an amateur myself. I was particularly anxious to hear his explanation of why, in Cairo, the United States is subject to more vitriolic attacks than either the British or the French, despite the fact that it was they who attacked Egypt in "armed aggression," while the United States saved Egypt through the United Nations condemnation. "There is some truth in that," said Mr. Hatem. "We were grateful to the United States when your President Eisenhower made his decision, in favor of living up to high moral principles, concerning the attack upon us rather than just sticking with old friends and NATO Treaty members. But I believe that one of the chief reasons why Egyptians are experiencing such strong feelings against the United States today is because they are enraged by the unfair, untrue attacks and insults against Egypt in the United States press."

Furthermore, it appears that while the British and French have been quite willing to negotiate such matters as the blocked Egyptian accounts, the United States is thought to be more adamant in these matters. Mr. Hatem offered other reasonable explanations of why Egypt has turned to the Soviet Union for weapons, drugs, and wheat. In his opinion, Egypt did not turn to Communism when it turned to Soviet Russia. As he pointed out, to be a Communist in Egypt is a crime punishable by fifteen years in jail. He repeated the theory of other Egyptian leaders, including President Nasser, that the Egyptians know how to distinguish between dealing with Russia and accepting any of the principles of Communism.

Regardless of explanations, I sensed here, as elsewhere in Egypt, that the bone of contention is our support of Israel, which is due to the Zionist influence in the United States in general. Egyptian leaders often recall an old Moslem saying: "Better a good word with no gift than a good gift with a bad word."

Emotional and intemperate as Egypt might often appear when it comes to foreign politics, it is less extreme than other young nations, if not moderate in its approach to welfare, social, and labor problems. In my talk with big, handsome, deliberate Hussein el Chafei, minister of social affairs and labor, I heard that Egyptian workers have enjoyed social security since it was introduced three years ago to all employees in companies employing fifty or more workers. The pattern recommended and operated by the government requires that the worker pay 5 per cent of his wages into the social security fund and his company 7 per cent. From the fund, the worker is guaranteed a certain amount of security through old age, along with accident and unemployment coverage. If the worker doesn't like the government plan he can choose some other of a dozen plans which are available and recognized by the government. The government plan was first applied in 1956 on a voluntary basis in Cairo and Alexandria, where 263 firms immediately participated. Now, about 77,000 laborers benefit from the government plan, while about the same number are covered by private insurance agencies. "The fund," explained el Chafei, "will provide the government with capital as well as organization for other social and welfare activities." The Egyptians have joined the International Labor Organization and are active in labor matters involving the League of Arab States. The Minister of Social Affairs and Labor seemed to feel that co-operation with these agencies was good but that Egypt had to solve its own labor problems.

Egyptian welfare does not start with housing problems according to el Chafei. Most Egyptians have no desire to junk their present mud dwellings and move into elaborate, modern apartment houses—even if they were available. "It must be borne in mind," said el Chafei, "that the vast majority of Egyptians live in rural rather than urban communities. They're satisfied with their houses and pleased with their gradual improvement."

After my visits to Ghana, the Belgian Congo, Kenya, and all of the North African countries, Egypt seems, by background, training, and capability, to be most ready to move forward in bettering the lives of its people if, to some degree at least, it can escape the emotional disturbances of the Middle East. The condition of the masses, which have been dreadfully poor and have suffered to no end in the past, is almost bound to improve. For this reason, it would seem that Egypt is a country where we can practice a hands-off policy. It is inconceivable that Communism can destroy the Moslem concepts of life or the Islamic religion, which would be a prerequisite for the Sovietization of Egypt. Many other foreign philosophies have been tried, but all have suffered dismal failure. It is, however, naïve for the Egyptians to think that they can separate the Soviet Union from Communist philosophy. If the Egyptians cannot save themselves from Communism, it is hardly possible for anybody else to save them.

Some observers argue that a few Egyptian deals with the Soviet Union might work as an efficient innoculation against Communism. If the Soviet Union wants to give Egypt money, supplies, or food, let them do it, these observers say. There is no better cure against Communism than the experience of its inefficiency in operation. There is no better protection against trust in business with the Soviet Union than to be stuck by them in small business dealings.

On the other hand, other and well-informed observers warn that our economic pressure on Nasser might well drive him—and with him the rest of the United Arab Republic—completely into the Soviet camp. That such a danger exists appears likely, and we would have to pay a very high price if such action came to pass: the oil which the Arab countries control. Arab oil is vital to European economic life, and Europe is an ally whose strength we must preserve.

This, then, is the threat of the Arabs. It is serious enough, although it is true that Egypt, let alone the other Arab countries, presents no direct military threat, as its disastrous defense in the Suez affair has shown. This complicates the question of economic aid, which we are willing to give to backward countries trying to get on their feet and to which Egypt certainly seems entitled. Subtle diplomacy, the readiness to assist, and the readiness to attach strings are needed. They will neither lose Egypt nor build it up as an enemy. These methods can be used only in intelligently measured portions, not as a prepackaged patent medicine.

8 Israel: Experiment and Energy

Many a Jew read as a child in the Old Testament: "If I forget thee, O Jerusalem, let my right arm lose its skill." Since ancient days, his Bible has reminded him: "How shall we sing the Lord's song in a strange land?" If he happens to be an escapee from the gas chambers of the Nazis or has suffered from the oppression of the Communists and the anger of the Arabs, he has come to find sanctuary in Israel. And many a young Jew from the cities of the world has gone to Israel to share in the adventure of pioneering with the people of his ancestry.

What Jews feel when they arrive in Israel may resemble the thrill I sensed the first time I sailed into the Irish port of Cobh and heard the bagpipes of which my grandfather had told me. Englishmen coming home from abroad know a similar happiness when they plow up the mad March Channel and can recognize the dim outlines of the chalk cliffs of Dover. And something similar is happening to your backbone when, after a long stay away from home, you see again the torch held high by the Statue of Liberty in New York Harbor.

Impressed by the continuous publicity drives for Jewish charity funds in New York City, many people think of the vibrating land of Israel as a tin-cup economy and a beggar's state rather than the independent nation of very independent individuals that it is today—without even the word "sir" in its language. Of course, the professionally promoted charity drives in the United States, which produce well over $100,000,000 annually, serve their goal. The pleading, starving eyes of a refugee on a poster will bring in more money than the healthy brown face and sparkling eyes of a happy Israeli child, yet you will see more children of this latter type. The children of the hundreds of thousands of refugees who arrive in Israel soon change under the benevolent care of the government, the rich means provided by American generosity, the warm sunshine of this Mediterranean republic, and the contagious enthusiasm of a vigorous people.

When I went to Jerusalem, I saw a marked contrast between the new Israel and the old, for Jerusalem is a divided city. The Arabs won't speak to the Jews, and the Jews can't speak to the Arabs. In the Arab section of Jerusalem, I found rocks and religion, while on the Jewish side, I faced a modern state, bridging, in one full sweep of ten years, centuries of history. On both sides are the same streets and hills through which Christ once walked with his message of peace and which are darkened today by the clouds of war. On one side, you see the overworked donkey of the Arab; on the other, the overworked Chevrolet of the Jew. You meet women with eyes downcast on the Arab side and people with chins up on the Israel side. On one side, men walk hand in hand; on the other, boys and girls laugh together. On one side are the rocky hills of Gethsemane; on the other, the fertile, irrigated fields of modern Israel.

In Israel, we find many answers to that old question, "What is a Jew?" If you believe that Jews can't farm, visit this land and see how well they do it. If you believe they lack fighting ability, look at Israel's well-trained, disciplined citizen-soldiers, who in one hundred hours defeated the regular army of Egypt. If you think they are not craftsmen, examine the magnificent embroidery of the Yemenites. If you think a Jew looks this way or that way, you'll be surprised to see in Israel the big-nosed, dark-skinned Jews of India and the blue-eyed, fair-skinned native sons next to the people of many other races and nationalities, from Chinese to Greek.

There are only 12,000,000 Jews in the world today. Six million live in the United States, 1,700,000 in Israel, 3,000,000 in the U.S.S.R., 500,000 in England, the rest in France, Germany, the Middle East, and elsewhere. They are all welcome in Israel, and many have settled there, usually in floods after new persecutions in one part of the world or another—the Russian-Polish pogroms, Hitler's campaign of extermination, the Communist persecutions, the North African–Arab squeeze. Ninety thousand came, with little or no possessions, to Israel during 1957. "You're already crowded. Your numbers are ahead of your economy. What are you going to do with all the new ones?" I asked one of the Israeli ministers. "We don't see it that way," he answered. "First, we welcome them, then we figure out how to care for them in temporary displacement camps until they can enter the organized society of the country."

At present, the economy of Israel labors under a heavy strain because the Arab countries have imposed an economic blockade. Today, it is impossible to sell Israeli goods to neighbor nations and buy Arab wheat in return, but Israeli Prime Minister David Ben-Gurion believes this difficult situation is, "in a way, all for the best, as it forces us to develop further our self-sufficiency. We will have to turn the wilderness of Negeb into a fruit-producing part of our agricultural economy to make up for what we cannot trade with our neighbors."

The 1,700,000 Jews in Israel occupy 7,800 square miles of territory. Most of it is fruitful, fertile, and productive land, largely because of good soil and extensive irrigation. "Which economic future do you foresee for Israel?" I asked David Horovitz, director of the Bank of Israel and an old-line Zionist. "Do you have a gadget that's going to solve all your problems, an aluminum-making hydro-electric dam such as the government of Ghana wants or a High Aswan Dam to improve agriculture such as the Egyptians plan?"

"No," he answered, "we have no single solution to our problem, but rather a whole series of different ways to increase our national income. For instance, each year we send more than $25,000,000 worth of commercial diamonds to the United States after they have been finished by skilled hands here. Unfortunately, however, the finishing process increases the final sale price by only 20 per cent. Or we sell oranges to England and France. This is already a $50,000,000 annual business, and it's expanding."

With intelligent work and inventiveness along these lines, Israel's national income is being increased each year but it does not suffice. Help is needed for refugees and for capital investment, much of which comes from America by way of the United Jewish Appeal and the Israel Bond Drive. It runs to $130,000,000 or more a year, besides the direct grant in aid from the U.S. government of $20,000,000 a year and $4,000,000 worth of surplus agricultural stocks.

Many individual Jews receive their share of indemnification and restitution for Hitler's crimes against them from the government of free West Germany, and the state of Israel itself is being paid a very substantial amount of "reparations," mainly in the form of machinery, ships, and other invaluable goods, by the West Germans. During the times of hardship that Israel has undergone in recent years, these large gifts from Germany have contributed a great deal—probably the decisive share—toward saving the country from crisis. Next to American voluntary donations, the German contribution must be credited for laying the foundation of Israel's future.

Israel must import wheat with substantial subsidies in order to place its retail price within reach of all. With this exception, its production of all other foodstuffs is already self-sufficient. According to Mr. Horovitz, who refuses to dream of a coming bonanza in oil, the future of Israel is based on its development in the areas of industry. Like Switzerland, which is also small and yet, thanks to its skill in the production of machinery, watchmaking, and other precision industries, is a rich little country or like England, which has always driven on its commerce, Israel is confident that it will find its own way toward prosperity, and I am inclined to share this optimistic view.

The real wealth of Israel is its youth. I seldom saw old people; perhaps they stay out of sight at home, but it is more likely that only the young and vigorous were able to endure the hardships of getting to this promised land. I did not notice any derelicts, beggars, or loafers. The hundreds of young men and women, deeply tanned by the sun and often clad in the brown uniforms of the Israeli army, are full of pep and confidence. "I never saw

Jews like these," one visitor from New York remarked. "They look as though they'd spent their lives playing tennis in the Catskills. Where do they come from?" They come from everywhere. From 1950 to 1956, for example, 36.9 per cent of the new arrivals came from Asia, 31.6 per cent from Africa, 30 per cent from Europe, and 1.5 per cent from America, and since 1957, they have been coming from Egypt and Morocco by the thousands. Right now, thousands more are escaping the Communist purgatory in Poland and Hungary.

You won't be in Israel very long before you meet an extraordinary group of immigrants, the Yemenites. They come from Yemen, a small spot on the faraway tip of Arabia, and are the purest of the Israeli Jews. They fled Palestine centuries ago when the invading Assyrians, Babylonians, and others destroyed their temples. They differed from other Jews in the complete retention of their ancient culture, their language, and their adherence to the Bible, despite pressures from foreign peoples around their small country. Until a couple of years ago, they had never seen an automobile, ridden on a train, dreamed of such a thing as an airplane, or even learned about radio. Then one day, to this land and people, forgotten for centuries, came the word that Israel was free, that King David had returned. King David, as they saw him, was David Ben-Gurion, the prime minister of Israel.

"If King David is back and Israel is free at last, praise God. We will return to our homes," said the Yemenites, and off they started, sixty thousand strong, to walk across more than a thousand miles of unfriendly deserts populated only by Bedouins. There seemed no chance for the wanderers ever to arrive at their destination, but along the route, agents of the American Joint Distribution Committee, masquerading as Arabs and carrying an abundance of gold pieces, helped them by bribing many a Bedouin chief who without this would not have allowed them to pass. When the Yemenites finally arrived at the British protectorate of Aden, they were in bad physical condition. Ten thousand of them had died on the desert trek, and it was imperative that the survivors be flown from this port to appropriate camps closer to Jerusalem where medical care, food, and guidance could help them. They had to be transported by air over this last leg of their journey, but how to get these simple people into an airplane? The problem was solved with ease. "The Bible," one of the Yemenites leaders announced, "says that we will be borne to Zion on the wings of eagles. It must have meant these giant birds." "The Magic Carpet" was the name given to this operation. Now the Yemenites are in their new homes. To them, everything seems wonderful in Israel—whether a plow, a truck, a machine, or a new radio, it has been willed by the Lord and therefore must be accepted. Each year, despite their small numbers, they win quite a few state prizes for outstanding performances in craftsmanship.

All of the people who come to Israel don't come from such backward places. You might wonder, as I did, why a young man from a wealthy Viennese Jewish family would give up all in 1920 to emigrate to a far-off, little-known land called Palestine. "I came here," a prominent business leader of Tel Aviv explained to me, "because as a youth I got interested in the Zionist movement. My family thought I was silly, but the adventure appealed to me. When I got here, I went into a kibbutz. We lived a communal life in those days to work on our job of draining a swamp. I stood in water up to my armpits day after day, until we had completed our job. You'll see crops growing there now. Of course the worst part of it was, I got malaria, as happened to most of us. Since mine was worse, I was sent away to an improvised hospital to recover. That's where I met my wife. She had also been one of the worst malaria cases in her kibbutz. We've been happy ever since, so maybe it was all for the best."

"Why did I come here?" said another Israeli in answer to my question. "What choice did I have? I was only nine years old, and we lived in Berlin when Hitler opened his gas chambers and my parents fled to this country." This German-born Jew is now an official of the government. "My name is Schlomo Porat," he told me, "but it used to be, in Germany, Werner Freund. We changed everything when we came here. The past is dead." Young Porat attended the American University in Washington, studied also in

Boston, and is now director of files and records for the Israeli government. "All this financial compensation from West Germany for those among us who suffered under the Nazis will amount this year to over $30,000,000 paid out in Israel. It's a most welcome gift to me. I only had to prove that I spend this money to attend school in the United States. Had we been allowed to remain in Germany, I would have had my education at a German university. As it is, they will give me the maximum allowance, which is DM 10,000. That's roughly $2,500 and will enable me to make a down payment on my own apartment."

This public servant earns $180 per month from which $30 is deducted by the state for taxes and social security. That leaves him $150, and he bolsters it, as many another Israeli does in this active land, with an extra job. He teaches two classes in business administration at a near-by school and, by means of per diem allowances, travel allowances, and compensation, ekes out another $24. His wife, mother of twins, adds about $30 by teaching the neighboring children part time. "We don't charge them much," explained Porat, "because they are our friends." This doesn't seem like very much money, and it does take night-and-day scrounging and working, but Porat and his family seem happy and are probably happier than they might be elsewhere. "Why don't you live in America, where life is easier, or in South America?" I questioned him. "Maybe," he answered, "because here I am needed and feel wanted. I can do something, and I would rather be a big frog in a little pond than a little frog in a big pond. Perhaps part of the satisfaction comes from the excitement of participating in this great adventure."

Israel's best-known experiment in social reform is the kibbutz. In a kibbutz, a communal settlement, all property is collectively owned and all work is organized on a collective basis. The members supply their labor and in return are supplied with housing, crude clothing, education, and cultural and social services. There is a central dining room and kitchen in each kibbutz, and children, after birth, are housed in a separate building, usually the best on the premises. The kibbutzim range from extreme Left

Wing groups of youths who have rebelled against the established order of their superiors to large communities which almost approach private enterprise.

A friend of mine, Francis Clifford Leffler, and I visited two youth kibbutzim, one in the north, near Galilee, and the other in the south, on the border of the much disputed Gaza Strip. Both were small and comparatively new, three years old at most. The oldest of the sixty members of one kibbutz was twenty-four, while the youngest said she was nineteen, but she looked much younger. The two camps are located just inside the Israeli border, one facing Jordan, the other Egypt. During the day, the occupants till their fields, but during the night, they guard their crops and their lives. Sooner or later, boys and girls appear before a rabbi to get married. Then, sooner or later again, the children start arriving, and that's when the kibbutz goes *kaput,* for the idea of separating all the babies in one building while the mothers work in the fields, the kitchens, and on guard duty does not seem to be very appealing. There is much agitation now against the custom of taking the children from their mothers.

With youngsters from sixteen to twenty-four freely intermingling in each kibbutz, their eventual marriage seems almost inevitable. For instance, in the kibbutz near the Gaza Strip, established three years ago and now consisting of fifty boys and girls, twenty have already married, and fourteen children are playing in the nursery. Moralists who would look down at these youths' chaperoning should recall that although the birth rate in Israel is one of the highest in the world, thirty-two per thousand, illegitimacy sets a low record, and immoral birth control is practically unknown.

There are, in all of Israel, approximately two hundred such camps. The members constitute less than 4 per cent of the total population, but many lessons of communal life can be and have been drawn from these kibbutzim, some of which have been in existence for fifty years or more.

On the opposite scale of economic organization, I found free enterprise at its best in Israeli developments. I visited a real American-type real-estate community development using African

capital and American suburban technique. Called Askelon-on-
Sea and part of the Afridar Housing Corporation, its investments
and the development itself are private, while the land is leased
from the government. The sign at the road entrance reads: "Fine
residence sites—Suitable industrial sites—Best in Askelon-on-
Sea." In the fine restaurant, I ate roast beef for eighty cents, while
hot dogs cost seventy cents. Besides the spick-and-span new
homes, the development contains a theater, a beautiful sand
beach on the Mediterranean, and a near-by cement-pipe factory.
The state of Israel is willing to permit all these different types of
home and real-estate developments, from socialist-planned col-
lectives to free-for-all private enterprise; the experimental spirit
behind it is one of "let's see how it works."

Israel has been trying to get on its feet since, eleven minutes
after its inception on May 14, 1948, President Truman, on behalf of the United States, recognized the newly established republic. A matter of hours later, the last of the British troops
withdrew, and the armed legions of the Arab world attacked the
new state, which had been carved and conquered and taken
away from the territories that had been settled by Arabs for
many centuries. Almost a million Arabs were driven from their
properties. The Israelis declared themselves the new owners of
everything they found in the land.

The battles didn't last long. The war, which Israelis have come
to call their war of liberation, ended with an armistice on February 24, 1949, and that's where the situation still stands—a state
of war still exists. Therefore, the Israelis explained that their
attack on the Suez in October-November, 1956, was only a continuation of that war. With the British and French joining in, the
sudden end of that campaign, the strangest ending in history,
may keep tacticians, diplomats, and historians scratching their
heads for centuries. It has, however, led to an end of border
raids by Egyptian-trained feyadeen and counter-reprisal raids by
Israeli troops. Now, all along their border, sitting lonesome in
their tents, are the observation forces of the United Nations.

I drove down to one of the check points in the Gaza Strip
where United Nations guards from India were sweating it out in

the hot shelter of their tents. They were not very cheerful. As they explained it, there is nothing for them to do in the town of Gaza, nor can they cross over to Jerusalem for a weekend. All they can do is sit there, perspire, and condemn their luck for an idleness which may or may not be producing worth-while results. The feyadeen stopped raiding because their strongholds were destroyed by Israeli attacks; in turn, the Israelis do not cross the border for reprisal raids because they would not find anything or anybody against whom to reprise. Because Secretary-General Hammarskjold of the United Nations has indicated that these United Nations guards are on Egyptian territory by permission of the Egyptian government of Colonel Nasser, the Israel punsters refer to UN as meaning "Under Nasser."

Today, although economic blockade by the Arabs continues, countered by Israel's increased activity in farming, industry, and trade, the war is in an uneasy stage of economic and political sparring, with military inactivity on the front but intensive action and counter-action behind the scenes. In this restrained war, psychological warfare is running at full blast out of Cairo, mainly through broadcasts from two stations. For their part, the Israelis are increasing the power of the "Voice of Israel" station from 50,000 kilowatts to 100,000 kilowatts. The mission of the Cairo stations is to unite the entire Arab world in a united front to destroy Israel. In turn, the aim of the "Voice of Israel" is to convince the Arabs that Israel wants peace and friendship. At the same time, the Israeli station tries to drive a wedge between Nasser's Egypt and the other Arab countries.

It looks to me as though in the long run, the Israelis will do a more professional propaganda job. The Egyptians seem rather inept in their indifference to public relations, their annoyance with the Western press, and their radio ragings. The Israelis, on the other hand, show much interest in public relations; they have constructed one of the finest modern buildings in Tel Aviv for the exclusive use of the press. For their radio programs to the Arab world, they have, as adviser, a man who is a product of the better Palestine Jewish-Arab relationships of old. His name is Ezra Denin, and his grandparents came to Palestine more than 120 years ago from central Europe. He was raised in an Arab village where he and his family were the only non-Arabs. He therefore knows the Arabs as few living men do and seems to have been successful at everything he ever tried his hand at, from the development of orange groves to fish ponds.

According to this expert's advice, the psychological warfare of the Israelis must exude common sense and persuasion and appeal to the moderation of the ordinary Arab without violent denunciations of the Arab leaders. How this is practiced was shown by one of the daily commentators who speaks perfect Egyptian Arabic, since he is a refugee Jew who was born and raised in Egypt as a member of the 2500-year-old Jewish community in Cairo. Calling himself "The Shopkeeper," he reports, for instance, on captured Egyptian soldiers, how they were well treated and shown Israel, including villages occupied by the 170,000 Arabs still living among the Jewish majority. And he made Egyptian soldiers themselves report what they saw and how it differed from what they had been told about Israel. An old technique which was widely applied during the war in Europe, it makes for good, believable, effective propaganda.

Another daily and equally moderate spokesman is called "David the Courier." He never answers an attack coming out of Cairo but some weeks later covers the subject by giving the facts as seen from his corner. He will admit the badness of an Israeli offense against the Arabs and mention the apologies of reparations offered by the Israeli government to the offended Arabs. "This was a terrible thing, a deplorable thing," he will say, "but let us not forget . . ." and then he lists crimes committed by the Arabs against the Israelis which were not compensated for or even apologized for. The Israelis are past masters in the art of persuasion.

Fear of Israel's increasing population and her need for expansion have motivated some of the Egyptian actions, I often heard in Cairo. Therefore I asked a number of Israeli leaders if their economic problems could be solved by a war of expansion, which would bring them additional territory from neighboring Arab states. The answer was a unanimous "No." The reason, I learned, was that there is no profit for Israel in an attempt to take desert lands. "We have too much of that in the south of Israel already," they said, "and we couldn't possibly take the Middle East oil, since we would run smack into American interests and perhaps precipitate a war with the Soviet Union. Even if we occupied territories of our neighbors, their population is so large, while ours is so small, that we would be unable to control those lands. World opinion and the restraining power of larger countries would make such action impossible. Finally, and most important, an aggressive war for the sake of expansion would destroy our idea of Israel, which was established to give refuge to our people and to enable us to develop our culture and heritage in peace."

Forty-three-year-old General Dayan, commander in chief of the Israeli army and the only general in the entire army at the time of my visit, has been busy setting up a powerful military establishment whose value was tested in the Suez campaign. His small army of approximately fifty thousand can be expanded overnight when reserves are mobilized. General Dayan is young, intelligent, competent. His trade-mark, a black patch over the empty socket of his left eye, was acquired in Syria when he fought with Australian troops against the Vichy French. A leader of the Zionist underground forces in Palestine, the Haganah, he has fought the Arabs, as well as the British, who captured Dayan in 1939, along with the class he was teaching in the underground's military school, and sentenced him to ten years in prison. But after one and one-half years in jail, the British released him to help them fight the war in Syria.

"General, could you have gone on to Cairo in the Suez attack?" I asked him. "We could have," he said, "but we had no intention of doing that. Our mission was accomplished. Our mission was to eliminate the feyadeen strong points which had been threatening and operating against Israel." I wondered whether it was his plan to let the Egyptian army escape. "Yes," he stated, "that was our order—to take the strong points and to drive the Egyptians out, but without undue risk to Israeli lives. We wanted to accomplish this mission with a quick victory and thus create a *fait accompli*."

I asked General Dayan what lessons his army had learned from the fight against the Egyptians. It had been such a short fight, he thought, that very few things had been learned which were not already known. But future defensive actions on the part of Israel, he added, might well be influenced by the future actions of the Soviet Union taken directly or by the Arab states with Soviet guidance in the Middle East. In General Dayan's view, the British bombardment of Egyptian airfields helped the Israeli forces a great deal, while in the first two days of fighting, the Egyptian planes did not take to the air at all. If they did any bombing of Israeli positions, it must have been very haphazard, for no casualties were scored. After the fighting had been stopped, surveys of the territory indicated that some bombs may have been dropped near Israeli positions, but without careful aim.

David Ben-Gurion, prime minister of defense of the state of Israel, who prefers to be called simply "Mister," considers General Dayan his crown prince. When I met Ben-Gurion, it was five o'clock and had been a long hot day, but he wasn't tired, despite his seventy-one years. Ben-Gurion is a husky little man, and his face, with the fuzzy white hair sticking out straight above each ear, is more hated and feared by Arabs than that of any other Israeli. Given to Old Testament fury, he is responsible for the reprisal raids of the Jews against raids made into Israel by Arab guerrilla bands. As he sat quietly behind his big desk, his white shirt open at the collar, in his dull-brown suit and black shoes, there was nothing spectacular in his appearance. Behind him were maps of North Africa and southern Europe, with the small spot of Israel indicated in correct proportions. At his right hand was a Bible and underneath it a great reference book in which all words of the Bible are catalogued, classified, and indexed. "When I want to quote the Bible, I look for it first in this reference book, then in the Bible itself," he explained.

"Mr. Prime Minister," I said to him, "you have sometimes been called the Jewish Churchill. That reminds me of a talk I once had with Clement Atlee; he had just defeated Winston Churchill and was British prime minister. When I told him that both he and Churchill were popular in America, he said: 'I also like Winston very much, but he reminds me of an historical layer cake. When you cut down into him, you never know to what century you will come.' But it seems to me," I said to Ben-Gurion, "that you usually know what century you're in, which would make you different from Churchill." "Yes," Ben-Gurion laughed and nodded, "the way we live here, I not only must know what century I'm in, but I must know what year, what month, what day, and even what hour!"

"Is it true what your enemies say—that you like to fight?" I asked him. "Perhaps I should not say this to a general," he answered, "but I really do not like fighting, nor do I even like the military. However, all my life, I've had to fight; I've had no choice in the matter. Fifty years ago, in these fields of Palestine, I had to carry a gun to work. One of my two best friends was shot beside me. That was in the days of Turkish rule of Egypt, but there was actually no rule at all—it was chaos in the main and we had to protect ourselves." I noticed that tears came into Ben-Gurion's eyes when he talked of his old comrade who was killed.

I inquired how he felt about the counter-raids and reprisals, which he had favored before the fighting in Sinai. "They were necessary," he said very briefly. Then he explained: "When our ordinary civilian farmers were killed on the border, we raided military units, such as the feyadeen headquarters across the borders. Most of these raids against us came from the Gaza Strip and from the border of Jordan."

"In that event," I said, "why was the attack in the southern direction across the Sinai Peninsula necessary?" Ben-Gurion answered: "We Jews don't want that country, but the Egyptians had organized feyadeen headquarters and were directing operations against our citizens from the Sinai Peninsula. We had to seize and destroy these organized centers. Actually, there's no one living in the Sinai Peninsula except a few tribes, but the people in these headquarters could have become real trouble-makers for us."

"Why didn't you go on to Cairo, Mr. Prime Minister?" I asked. "Reports would indicate that the Egyptian army was in full retreat. If you went on to Cairo, perhaps you could have terminated all of the difficulties which now continue." Ben-Gurion extended his right hand and put it on the Bible. "The Bible said twenty-two centuries ago, 'Do not return to Egypt.' So why should we go back?"

"Why, then, did your army stop short of the Suez Canal?" I inquired. "You, an American general, ask me why we stopped!" he snapped back. After a broad grin, he continued: "We had accomplished our mission and got the British ultimatum to stop. The British had by then received Russian threats and were also deterred by the United States' attitude." It seemed to be Ben-Gurion's idea that the British, with their sixty thousand troops, and the French, with their thirty thousand troops, both with orders to spare no lives or equipment to accomplish their mission, could have completed the conquest of Egypt or the overthrow of Nasser in a matter of four days. So why did *they* stop? "Do you think, Mr. Ben-Gurion, that the British and French stopped because they really believed that the U.S.S.R. would bomb London and Paris?" "I think," said he, "that the American position was more important to them."

"What do you think of American foreign policy in this and other matters? Is it good?" I asked. "What *is* the American foreign policy?" he countered. "The way I'd judge it," I said, "it amounts to about the following: the United States offsets the U.S.S.R. so that they will not begin World War III. At the same time, we encourage both Israel and Egypt in their efforts to improve themselves." "If that's the policy," said Ben-Gurion, "it's good. We do not hate the Egyptian people. We want them to prosper too."

"An Egyptian minister told me," I continued, "that the relationship between Israel and Egypt has now returned to the conditions of 1947. If Israel wants peace, it must withdraw from the lands which it has taken from the Arabs after that date." "How could we?" demanded Ben-Gurion. "We will give up these lands when the Arabs give back the lives of the Israelis killed by Arab attacks against us. The Arabs abandoned their farms to enlist in these attacks against the Jews, and only after this did we settle our refugee families on these farms; today, it is too late to talk about withdrawing to the lines of 1947." Ben-Gurion recalled: "In 1948, all the military experts advised that Israel had no chance against the combined forces of the Arabs then about to attack us. How could the population of Israel, which then numbered only six hundred thousand, stand up to the armies of about thirty-four million Arabs? All we had was the Haganah, our defense force, but with practically no guns, little equipment, and not much training. What we had was our spirit, and we discovered that this decided the victory. The Arab soldiers didn't know why they were fighting. We knew. *We were fighting for our lives!*"

From then on, our conversation proceeded to many other questions. I asked: "What do you visualize as the solution to your Arab-Egypt problem?" Ben-Gurion was quick to respond: "Time and patience. I used to think that Nasser would change, but I was mistaken. We must wait and work. His people will finally reject him because he does not truly represent them. Egypt should be developing its own country and economy rather than spending its time, money, and energies on military adventures in an attempt to rule the Arab world. While we wait for Nasser's downfall, we will continue to make good use of our time and develop the state of Israel in peaceful growth."

"What about the one million Arab refugees?" I asked. "What would you do with them?" Ben-Gurion's answer was: "They could all go to Iraq, where they would be most welcome. Two rivers make the land of Iraq fertile. The population is small. They need help. These Arabs would fit into the economy. Or they could all settle in the south, on the edge of the Sinai Peninsula, where, with energetic work, they could develop a fertile land."

Howley: "Do you think the people of Iraq would accept the one million Arab refugees or a large part of them?"

Ben-Gurion: "They probably wouldn't because they wouldn't dare offend Nasser, and Nasser wants these refugees to remain a troublesome problem."

Howley: "What about the Arab blockade of Israel?"

Ben-Gurion: "In a way, the Arab blockade is good for us, although it imposes additional hardships on us. The Arabs try now to make it prohibitively expensive to maintain Israel against their trade barriers and blockades. But as a response, we develop our own economy and become more self-sufficient. First, they tried to wipe us out, when thirty-four million Arabs attacked six hundred thousand Israelis. But they failed in their effort to destroy us by war. Then they tried to disorganize us with terror raids on our citizens and with organized guerrilla activities against our people. This, too, did not succeed. Now we have this Arab-imposed economic blockade. I admit that it makes things difficult for us; we would prefer trade with the Arab countries to our mutual advantage. But since we cannot buy food from the Arab countries and sell them our products, we will respond to the challenge again and develop the wilderness of the Negeb Desert as another long step towards the economic betterment of Israel."

When I said good-by to Ben-Gurion, he answered, "Shalom," and added: "Do you know what that means, General?" "Yes, I know," I said. "It means 'Peace.' "

On leaving Ben-Gurion, and soon thereafter his country, I wondered whether we can take a stand according to general principles (which are often no more than high-sounding clichés) in our relationships with foreign countries. The reason for my wonderment is that these principles, admirable and valid though they are as such, rarely fit the given situation in a foreign country. In this regard, Israel seems to resemble Algeria. Both sides have a good point in favor of their position. The French, like the Jews, came to Algeria by right of conquest and settled there. The Arabs have lived in Israel since time immemorial, and they see the Jews, just as the Algerians see the French, as invaders. On the other side, the Jews and French have lived, built, worked, and become part of Israel and Algeria. Whether one approves of the past or not, the past cannot be undone, nor would it be right to undo present achievements and future prospects.

It seems to me that it would be wiser for our foreign policy to stick only to the direct interests of the American people and interfere abroad only where American interests—the defense interest in particular—is concerned. As the Soviet Union prepares its war of world conquest, we must block and check its advances, but when it comes to Arabs and Jews, we cannot take sides. All we should do—and sensibly can do—is to let both peoples profit from our sympathies, support, and experience if and while they struggle to improve the lot of their peoples in peaceful ways, without force and violence.

9 Middle East: Following the Middle of the Road

The Middle East, meeting place of Europe and Asia and the cross-roads of Africa and Eurasia, has become the great testing ground of American foreign policy. In fact, during the recent past, the Middle East has come to be an almost perfect laboratory in which to test our middle-of-the-road policy for its strength, as well as for its weakness. But then the Middle East is much more than a mere testing ground. It is a decisive battle-field of the Cold War, and our defeat there could well mean our loss of Europe and probably a world-wide contest with the Soviet Union.

At first glance, it might seem that our policy in the Middle East has been confused, unguided, and highly erratic. At one time, we merely used words; at another, we acted. And our words, as well as our actions, were sometimes based on the principles of absolute morality, at other times on the principles of practicality, if not expediency. One day we supported Israel against the Arabs; the next day we upheld the Arabs against Israel. Now we would come to the aid of democracies; then we would assist feudal systems against more popular movements. At one given moment, the goal of our middle eastern policy seemed to be to please some American voters and to win a coming election, while at other times the interest of American oil investments appeared to be the guiding light. Of course, our words, as well as our actions, must be keyed clearly and exclusively to the requirements of the American national self-interest; and American business, European business, oil interests, and quite a few other interests are part and parcel of our national interest if and when they are balanced against each other. It is in these terms that we must judge, and deal with, the Middle East, as with every other foreign area.

One reason for our seemingly erratic and unprincipled policy in the Middle East is that this area lacks unity in itself; its composition is as piecemeal as our foreign policy appears to be. No common and general yardstick can be applied to an area whose parts are as widely divergent from each other as are, say, the peoples and governments of the American continents from Canada to the tip of South America. A second reason is that by the end of 1958, we had to deal with Nasser's United Arab Republic, consisting of Egypt and Syria; we also had to deal with the nations that had joined the Baghdad Pact in order to contain Soviet Russia on its southern border—Turkey, Iran, Pakistan, and, at the end of 1958, an uncertain Iraq. Third, we have had to give serious thought to our relationship with the kingdom of Jordan. Fourth, there remain our ties with Israel.

To make the crazy quilt seem a little crazier, a major role was played by the League of Arab States, which partly overlapped with this political line-up and tried to unite the Arabs from the Persian Gulf to the Atlantic in a peaceful manner. If there was to be violence, the League preferred to leave it to the discretion of its member states. With each of these nations, or groupings of nations, whose interests or aims often sharply contradicted each other, a different way of American policy was required, unless we identified ourselves with only one of them and were prepared to let the others go, and this we surely could not and cannot do.

We could spare ourselves this walk on the middle eastern tightrope if it were not for the oil which marks much of the area. Oil has washed away the traditional middle eastern ways of thinking and living, thereby creating a vacuum for new forces to enter. In the era B.O., that is, "Before Oil," the Arab peoples had lived according to Mohammed's teachings; personal progress and material improvement meant little, while man's inner integrity was the only worthy goal. If this seemed a proper philosophy for people who dwelled in sandy wastelands and could not aspire to worldly goods, they had to change it for a new outlook toward new ideas, new powers, and new ways of life when oil emerged from their lands.

Today, more than forty-eight million Arabs from Iraq to Egypt, from Saudi Arabia to Lebanon, from Iran to Jordan crave the material advantages that are waiting for them under their soil in the form of almost limitless oil resources. They are well aware that this treasure-dream come true—at the rate of five and one-half million barrels a day bubbling forth from their barren soil—supplies more than one-fifth—23 per cent, to be exact—of the world's vital needs. And the Arabs know that they can control the very lifeline of Europe, which is as dependent on their oil as is America on Europe's economic and military strength.

While this sudden wealth descended on previously starving nations, and while the hope for a personal share in this wealth carried away almost every citizen, it was not surprising that the desire for a new order—with prosperity at home, as well as power in the international sphere—became a popular middle eastern dream. To make this dream come true, the Arabs set out on an aggressive search for a powerful leader who would translate their dream into reality; they well remember that their past glories have always depended on the coming of such a leader—from the Persian kings who invaded Europe to Mohammed himself. In a way, President Gamal Abdel Nasser of Egypt aims to be this new, though strictly secular, Mohammed of our time, and he has shown that he is a skillful manipulator of mobs, a clever politician when it comes to national aggrandizement, and a good hater.

What the "awakening Arab world" (the prospering Arab world might perhaps be a more accurate description) also looks for in addition to a new leader is a new sociopolitical system in which it can organize its new potential power. It is in this context that the Soviet Union sees its great chance to move in and wrest the area away from the West. The advent of Russia in the Middle East, an entirely new thing, contributes a great deal toward complicating the situation in that area. In the past, the growl of the

British lion had been strong enough to drive off Imperial Russia—under both the Czarist and Communist flags—and its direct, conspicuous advances. But today, Communist Russia tries to come in through the back door by what President Eisenhower has aptly termed "indirect aggression." With Nasser as their rather willing tool (Nasser sometimes seems to mistake the Soviets as his willing tool in uniting the Arab world and destroying the infidels of the 1958 crop), the Soviets have a good chance to infiltrate and infect the coveted area, and they use their chance accordingly.

Past masters at the art of starting trouble on the road to revolutions, the Russians have discovered assassination as a valuable weapon that is particularly useful to their needs in the Middle East. If Lenin rejected "individual terror," that is, the murder of individual members of the ruling class by individual revolutionaries, since it was "the system" rather than some of its representatives he wanted to overthrow, his principle does not apply to the Middle East. On the contrary, after half a dozen men leading a middle eastern nation are eliminated, its very "system" has disappeared, and the people will accept another group with another "system" as leaders, for good or for bad.

Murder as a political technique has ancient roots in the Arab world, as is demonstrated by the very word "assassination," which is derived from the Arab word *hashshashin,* referring to those addicted to hashish, a drug often given to men who were to kill someone on an Arab king's orders. Now, as then, it suffices for a ruler to give hashish to some of his subjects and have them kill his opponents. But a new kind of drug is favored in the process today; the contemporary middle eastern murderers are given the favorite contemporary hashish: to semi-intellectuals and mobs, in short, it's Soviet Communism.

Yet in addition to all of these disturbing factors, the middle eastern situation has become what it is today (and thereby poses its most difficult and dangerous problems to American foreign policy) because of the appearance of the new state of Israel on Middle-Eastern ground. Israel supplies the common denominator of Arab mass hatred, and hatred has proved to be a good instrument for goading people into action, for uniting them against a common enemy, for leading them anywhere.

In dealing with Israel, U.S. foreign policy has definitely moved down the middle of the road, which is often merely a way of saying that we have been playing both ends against the middle. At any rate, we have given up the Truman Administration's policy of wholehearted and complete support for Israel at the expense of our relationship with the Arabs. The main reasons for Truman's one-sided policy were explained to me by an official who himself played a leading role in shaping that policy. "The United States government," he told me, "is a representative government; that is, it represents the American people, its temper and aspirations, and also its foreign relations. The six million American Jews are an important segment, though a minority, of the American population. Since they are voters, and often leaders of industry, commerce, and banking, the voice of our foreign policy must reflect their interest and their desires as it reflects the vocal interests and desires of other groups in the United States. In turn, there are practically no Arabs in the United States. Therefore, we cannot be neutral when it comes to a choice between the Arab world and the country of Israel. We must choose Israel and support it."

The present administration has reversed this policy, since it believes that in the long run it is better for all the people of the United States not to antagonize the Arabs. Yet we cannot completely ignore that nation which we have done so much to encourage. We must therefore support both the aspirations of the Israelis and the aspirations of the Arabs, as Nasser has outlined them. It follows that our actions in the Middle East tend to be merely reactions to specific moves made by the other nations involved. For instance, after Israel, Great Britain, and France attacked Egypt, we opposed them and probably led them to halt operations before they had accomplished anything. Almost ironically, we joined our world-wide enemy, the Soviet Union, in the condemnation of France, Great Britain, and Israel—in other words, our oldest friend, our staunchest ally, and our special protégé.

If, even in the past few years, the policy of playing both sides of the middle eastern street—by political benevolence as well as by financial support given to both Israel and the Arab world at the same time—has turned out to be as difficult as keeping one foot on a boat and the other on the dock, a moment may come in which it would seem impossible to continue this attempt, which could well lead to war. Such a situation would almost necessarily arrive if, for instance, Israel's present request for admission to the Baghdad Pact were granted. The Arab world will attack Israel as soon as it feels ready to do so; if we are allied with Israel by a mutual assistance pact, we must come to Israel's aid. In turn, the Soviets, if they consider such a moment appropriate for their own aims, would line up with the Arab side, and the third world war might begin.

In the fall of 1958, a group called the United Zionist Revisionists of America, Inc., published advertisements in the New York press in which they exercised their right, as American citizens, to tell the people of the United States what they deemed an advisable foreign policy. "Israel has to be integrated," the advertisement stated, "into the mutual defense network of the free world. The United States must conclude a mutual security pact with Israel; the valiant army of the young State has twice routed the Arab aggressors; it is able again to stem Nasser's pan-Arabism, which is but the cutting edge of communist advance in the Middle East. Let the U.S. furnish the necessary weapons for Israel's defense and Nasser and his master, Khrushchev, will be stopped in their tracks; only thus will the world be freed from the spectre of a third global conflagration."

Surely a case can be made for a policy of choosing sides and perhaps a strong case can be made for this policy of choosing the side of Israel, but it would not be the present policy of the middle of the road, with its almost aggressive neutrality and friendship for all. If this has turned out to be a very rocky road, it holds out better hope than any other policy to lead America to its national goals.

This road along our policy line of the middle of the road gets no less rocky when we move across Israel's border into Jordan, with its equally difficult and dangerous problems. King Hussein, the ruler of this small country with the largest border that any Arab state shares with Israel, was held on his throne only by the presence of British troops and by the influx of American financial support. Somewhat paradoxically, the King was therefore forced to remain friends with Great Britain and America, who, in turn, were friends of Israel. Yet to maintain a modicum of popular following, the King had to join in the popular outcry, according to which "Israel must be destroyed."

This popular mood was demonstrated (and also explained) to me on a recent visit to Jordan when I was given a bodyguard to move through its cities. The giant Arab legionnaire who was assigned to this job was indeed the only wall to protect me from insults and assaults as they had been directed against other Western visitors of that country only a short while before. The people who indulge in this hatred are Arab refugees who left their Palestinian homes during the war with Israel and fled to Jordan. Almost eight hundred thousand of these refugees now constitute more than one-half of the entire Jordanian population. Because of this, the country, thoroughly shaky in its economics, runs up an annual deficit of seventy-five million dollars.

I talked with quite a few refugees in their camps, and there seemed little doubt that they would remain an eternal source of international friction, no matter how hard the United Nations tries to better their lives. At the camp of Dheisheh, for instance, I found five thousand refugees, among them five hundred children under sixteen. All were fed sixteen hundred calories a day. Most of them lived in new ten-by-ten-foot concrete boxes with dirt floors—only a few had concrete floors on which to put sleeping mats—whose single room served as home for an entire family. The majority of the camp inmates were older people, and they sat around all day long thinking only of the day when they could go back home to Israel. I asked a grandfather who took care of half a dozen children orphaned by the death of his daughter and son-in-law what his greatest wish would be if Allah were to promise him its fulfillment. Without a moment's thought, he answered: "That I could return to my home." His home, of course, was the place where he was born and raised and where he expected to die, in what is now Israel. Particularly the older Arabs have no other choice, since they lack the gift of many Irishmen or Jews to move to different parts of the world, adjust themselves quickly, and make their way in the new country. Valiantly though the United Nations officials work in these camps to teach trades to their inmates, to find them jobs near by, and to battle all those diseases which threaten displaced persons and which I remember well from my own wartime work, they have not much hope for another solution but the return to their old homesteads.

For us, there is little else to do now but to continue the support of these refugees through the United Nations, to try to keep King Hussein on his throne, and to hope that Nasser will not succeed in upsetting the Israeli-Jordanian truce. In this case, we might uphold the *status quo* for the foreseeable future. But if, for instance, King Hussein and some of his followers be assassinated, as the radio voice of Nasser has been urging, the uneasy equilibrium would be upset overnight. In such a case, Israel would most probably feel compelled immediately to march into Jordan to secure the mountains as a natural defensive barrier against future Arab attacks. The middle of the road, too, has sharp turns, with new dangers and problems threatening around the corner.

There are no clear-cut, ready-made policy directions on the middle of the road, as we learned in another middle eastern country, Iraq, in the summer of 1958. True, only yesterday in Suez we had been shocked by the use of force by our friends and opposed it, but when, in Iraq, we were also shocked by the use of force, directed, for that matter, against our friends, we supported rather than resisted it. That was when power was seized by a small clique which contained notoriously anti-Western elements and which assassinated the King, the Crown Prince and the Premier of Iraq in a bloody, ruthless *coup d'etat*. In spite of indications of Communist influences behind the plotters and the well-organized street mobs that backed it, we recognized the new government with breakneck speed.

Unpleasant though this speedy recognition of the new government must have been to our policy-makers, they justified it in the American national interest. If we had failed to take this action, our policy-makers argued, the Communists would have gained an advantage, and perhaps power, in Iraq. Others doubted this assumption, since in the latter case the Iraqi government would have lost an annual oil revenue from the West amounting to two hundred million dollars, which the Soviets could hardly pay in our stead. Yet to keep in power and to appease the mobs which it has released, the new government could not forego this financial support; the new premier, Abdul Karim el-Kassem, has already cut rents, sliced the bread price, and reduced living costs in order to keep in the mob's good graces. Without "Western imperialist oil money," the socialist state, whose establishment the new Iraqi rulers have announced, could never be financed. This somewhat paradoxical need supplies our aces in the game. After we recognized his government, the new premier pledged not to rock the boat, but some of his associates have left little doubt that they have chosen Nasser's camp. The middle-of-the-road policy is forced to gamble, even when the odds look poor.

Like the Iraqi monarchy, President Camille Chamoun's government in Lebanon, whose people, descendants of the ancient Phoenicians, are considered the Middle East's smartest businessmen, had been counted among our most faithful friends. Yet when Chamoun's term in office expired in the summer of 1958 and civil war threatened to erupt over his successor, we speedily dumped him as a "controversial" figure after granting his last request in office by sending thirteen thousand U.S. troops to Lebanon. Our main purpose was to prevent a violent rebellion on the Iraqi pattern; another good reason was our understanding that the Middle East recognizes only force, is always ready to join the stronger side, and will always accept the biggest offer. Without this display of force, we, as well as the British, would have lost our standing in the Middle East.

One important side effect of our sending troops into Lebanon was that we learned much about the Soviet Union's intentions. In the same way that we came into Lebanon at the request of Chamoun, Soviet troops could have been sent there on a direct or volunteer basis at the request of the Lebanese rebel leader, whose government in the mountains might very well have been promptly recognized by the Communist countries. All kinds of excuses were available to the Soviets had they wished to take the first steps toward a world war over our "armed intervention" in Lebanon. Since the Soviets carefully abstained from all actions, it was impressively demonstrated that, at least for the present, the Soviet Union will not consider an all-out war, even on a limited part of the globe, a fact our foreign policy might well remember in other parts of the world. In the Middle East, as elsewhere, the Cold War continues on the economic, political, and psychological level, and the middle of the road seems best suited for the defensive holding operations which this area requires.

10 North Africa: Trouble Zone

If you draw a line on your map from Paris to Gibraltar to Tunis, it will show the shape of a "V." If we succeed in holding this line, it may well be a "V" that stands for our victory in the Cold War; if we let it slip from our grip, though, it is more likely to stand for our vanquishment. For along the "V" line from Paris to Gibraltar to Tunis are American air bases, with additional ones now under construction in Spain, which represent the investment of billions of American dollars. What is more, these bases, and the American soldiers and diplomats on the spot, carry a major responsibility for the security of the free world.

The Soviets are well aware of the importance North Africa holds in the defense of freedom. As they see it, he who controls the western Mediterranean is likely to control Europe, Africa, and perhaps the rest of the world. That is why they do their level best to shake the very ground on which our control of the area rests. The way for them to arrive at this is to spread terror and chaos throughout North Africa. If you turn on your radio anywhere and anytime in North Africa, you will hear Radio Budapest blaring at you: "Rise up, you Algerian patriots, and destroy your foreign exploiters." Turn the dial, and Radio Cairo will scream at you: "Every Moslem must kill a Frenchman—this is the only way to free your country."

These words are backed up by deeds. The Soviets smuggle rifles and grenades into the troubled area by land and by sea. Organizers, agitators, and active terrorists are trained in special military-political schools in Egypt, to be sent to Algeria, Tunisia, and Morocco after graduation. These schools, as a confidential report dispatched by the governor-general of Algeria to a member of the Paris government sets forth, "are set up at Cairo according to instructions from the chief of the Egyptian government and from the council of the revolution by special services of the Egyptian army; their job is to recruit, pay, issue passports to, and direct in general, the agents of the North African separatist movements. They train commandos with headquarters in which Tunisians, Algerians, and Moroccans are represented."

If North Africa appears as one unit as far as our military security and the Soviet campaign to undermine it are concerned, it is no unit at all when it comes to its own problems. Each of its major parts differs greatly from all the others, with problems all its own. The one thing that the majority of these people do have in common is their Moslem faith, but beyond that, there is no tie whatsoever which would bind them together. If you call a Moroccan an Arab or if you mistake an Algerian for a Tunisian, he will probably correct you by slicing your throat. As an Algerian assured me, "Tunisia is a woman, Algeria a man, and Morocco, a tiger."

ALGERIA

Politically, Algeria is as much a part of France as Puerto Rico is a part of the United States. Its area is four times that of metropolitan France, but it is certainly more than four times as complicated. Of its nine and one-half million citizens, one million are of European origin. Most of the Europeans are of French stock and were born and raised in Algeria, while others are of different European descent. Many are descendants of the hundreds of families who came to Algeria from Alsace-Lorraine after the Franco-Prussian War in order to avoid living under German control. The approximately two hundred thousand Jews of Algeria, have, in the main, retained their bloodlines and culture and are rightfully classified with the other Algerian-European groups. The rest of the people in Algeria, a mixture of many races, seem to be the product of history's melting pot, out of which came a human bouillabaisse. No one knows for sure just what to call those Algerians who are not of European origin. A mélange of more than twenty races, these "natives" cannot be accurately classified as Arabs, as is frequently done. Nor are they more "native" or "indigenous" than other Algerians; and they are not "brown" or Riffian. Since they contain a bit of all this, no title fits.

These Algerians are unified by the Islamic faith rather than by great leaders or great traditions. Islam established itself as the dominant religion in the seventh century when the conquering Moslems gave no choice but to "acknowledge Mohammed or die." Their conquest brutally abolished Christianity, which St. Augustine had worked so faithfully to establish in North Africa. When the French came in 1830, chaos, piracy, and savagery ruled the land. After a short, hard fight, the French approached the city of Algiers to be greeted by the heads of more than two hundred of their countrymen hanging from hooks on the walls. Algiers was in those days a malaria-infested swamp. The old city, called the Casbah, was then, as it still is now, a labyrinth of filth, fit only for very primitive inhabitants.

With the French came Europe's know-how. Order was established and justice imposed, and in the years that followed, a tremendous economic effort was set forth. Swamps were drained, cities built, and farms and factories set up throughout Algeria. The French brought 19,000 farm tractors to the lands. Three thousand miles of railroad were laid, and 52,000 miles of roads were built. New French-installed hospitals, with a total of 25,000 beds, and rural sanitation units cut the mortality rate from twenty per thousand to ten per thousand, while at the same time, the birth rate increased from twenty per thousand to thirty per thousand. Eight large hydro-electric dams were constructed to offset the irregular rains and to recover more than 510,000 acres of arid land; today, these water-power and coal-burning plants produce more than 900,000,000 kilowatt hours of electricity for expanding Algerian industry.

Algeria's present-day wealth is not based on natural resources, and in those areas where the French have not been very active, we find little economic progress. The Tuaregs, veiled camel

riders of the Sahara Desert, have changed little in their wild and
ancient ways since they swept across Africa and into Spain in
the seventh and eighth centuries. They might change quickly,
however, if the Shell Oil Company and others now drilling in the
Sahara—and preliminary drilling is encouraging—should strike
oil. But if today all the people of European origin were driven
out of Algeria in the same way that Hitler drove German citizens
of Jewish origin out of Germany, the blow to Algeria's political,
social, and economic life would be very serious for both Europe
and Algeria.

With the exception of the largest oil company, Tamzalo Cie,
which is owned by an Arab, almost every transportation, industrial, business, and sanitation company, even modern farming,
has been inspired and is guided by men of European origin. The
reason is not that the non-European in Algeria has been held
down. The real reason is that he just doesn't care for modern
progress. "If Allah wanted a bridge built there, he would have
created one," he will say. Or, "If Allah wanted a factory in that
field, he would have put one there instead of the lovely flowers
which he alone can create."

This Moslem attitude—one of the great handicaps of all progress in Algeria—stems from the fact that the ancient economic
and social interpretations of the Koran, the sacred book of Mohammed, are still accepted in all literalness today. But it seems
almost impossible to live up to its prescriptions and get ahead in
modern economic ways at the same time. Take, for instance, an
average laborer. For one whole month called Ramadan, he eats
and drinks nothing during the day, which leaves him too weak to
perform a hard day's labor. Seven times each day, starting at
4:30 in the morning, he must drop all other activities, face toward Mecca, and go through a prayer ritual requiring first the
washing of the right hand three times, then the washing of the
left hand three times, then the washing of the mouth three times,
and so on over the body, chest, and feet. If he is in the Sahara, he
may use sand instead of water. It seems that this washing, which
was good procedure in ancient, less hygiene-conscious days, is a
bit out of place in a modern world of running water. I asked one

Arab worker what he wanted and expected to get in heaven. His reply was: "Oh, a little pretty garden, with a few fruit trees." Sitting on a stone and contemplating the universe, he does not feel that he could realize his paradise on earth right now with only a little extra work.

Worst off by modern standards, of course, are the Moslem women. You can see them on every Algerian street, blinded with blinkers like animals and hardly much freer. They have learned to master only household chores and are carefully kept from contacts with the outside world. I have watched them with pity and fascination as they ventured to go shopping, wrapped from head to toe in many layers of sheets. With only one eye may such a woman peek at the vegetables she is going to buy, while at the same time she holds up her skirts, hangs on to her market basket, tries to protect her head wrapping from the wind, makes her choice, and reaches into the folds of her dress for her purse, where she finally finds a coin. Often enough, these women are married at eleven, have their first baby at twelve, and never speak to a man other than their husbands. When a Moslem woman goes to market to sell her wares, she must lead a three-foot-high donkey, on top of which rides happily her lord and husband.

This role of the Moslem woman as an outcast is of rather recent date. In the past, great women had arisen to lead their countrymen. They still remember Cahina, who by her wisdom, courage, and skill gained the following of all the Berbers; she led them to battle against the Arabs, whose line of conquest she broke in proud victories. She arrived at her powerful station late in life and was said to be 127 at her death. Cahina was by no means the only North African woman to lead her people. Some future day, the Moslem women might well come to imitate these leaders of the past again rather than remain yesterday's slaves, for they have already begun to break loose from their unhappy traditions. Today, smart Moslem ladies seen on the streets of the large cities still wear the veil, but it consists only of a very attractive triangle of transparent silk or lace, which can be removed at will. Likewise, the jalava, a loose, coat-like garment with a hood, is gradually replacing the much-folded, less practical garment known as the burnoose.

If many Moslem women are now rebelling against their traditional lot, so do many of their men rebel in many ways. People are beginning to adjust their thinking to the requirements of modern life. More than three hundred thousand laborers from North Africa, after working in France, have brought back not only money but also new ideas. Children of both European and North African origin now attend the same tolerant French schools, where they acquire knowledge not to be gained in the traditional Moslem schools, whose methods of education often consist only of memorizing the writings of the Koran forward and backward, while higher education exhausts itself in debate on the exact interpretation and meaning of these writings. Moslem men who have been educated in French schools and who have gone to universities in Paris told me they are no longer willing to accept the teaching that the world is flat. Moslem farmers observe from European-controlled farms near by that the time and effort spent by others to improve the land, to fertilize the crops, and to till scientifically produces more grain, more grapes, and more vegetables.

It is this evolution which the Communists have turned into a violent revolution. In the great social adjustments which are taking place and which modern communications are speeding up, the Communists see their chance to precipitate violence in what could well develop in normal, peaceful ways. For this purpose, they have found native troublemakers, such as Messali Hadj. He has been a rebel almost since he was born in May, 1898, at Tlemcen. The dossier of his crimes from 1934 until now covers ten pages of closely typed recordings. (The French are very good at keeping track of criminals, even though they are reluctant to do anything about them.) At present, he is working with the Egyptian Moslem "Brotherhood," co-operating with the Communist Party of France, and seeking, in the usual Communist manner, to gain leadership of dissatisfied elements in North Africa. Not only has he appealed for his cause in a letter to President Eisenhower, he also operates, in New York City, a mysteriously financed committee of liberation which advertises in American newspapers. That these advertisements in support of terrorism appear not only in the *Daily Worker,* which would be understandable to our French allies, but also in the *New York Times* struck the French resident-general of Algeria as little short of incredible, as he and others often told me.

Another self-appointed "liberator," Si Messaoud, one of the chief rebels in the south of Constantine, issued to his followers this appeal (which was captured by the French): "All utilities, mosques, schools, houses of the enemy must be destroyed. . . . Destroy the telegraphic lines and attack those who repair them. . . . Take no prisoners except the top leaders. . . . Continue to burn farms and all the houses of the Goums. . . . Have no pity for the families of Moroccans. . . . The women, the Colonials, and the French civilians must be killed. . . . Kill the traitors and the isolated suspects in the villages by suicide commando raids. . . . Kill the followers of Bourguiba, the Tunisian traitors. . . . Our independence will come through violence."

Naturally, such inflammatory advice, backed up by arms and Communist organizations, leads the wild Berbers in the hills and the dissatisfied elements in the cities to go on sprees of death and devastation. Many of their murders were committed with barbarous cruelty, as, for instance, in the massacre near the mining village of Philippeville on August 20, 1955. Enraged by propaganda appeals to kill, mountain men rushed upon the village to kill every member of the fifty French families working at the mines, as well as all the non-Europeans with them. Throats were sliced and bodies mained in a scene of incredibly cruel horror.

In 1957, French Foreign Minister Christian Pineau reported to the United Nations Political Committee of the General Assembly that "between November 1, 1954, and December 1, 1956, 5,344 civilians, men, women and children were assassinated." Mr. Pineau accused Egypt and the Soviet Union of indirect participation in the terror. "It is Egypt," he stated, "acting to some extent under Soviet inspiration which has given the Algerian rebellion the most continuous and effective support." An understanding of Egypt's part in causing deaths and chaos in Tunis,

Algiers, and Morocco makes more understandable France's willingness in November, 1956, to join Great Britain and Israel in
punitive action against Nasser.

During all of this, the outlawed Communist Party of Algiers
was in contact with the Communist Party of France, a party which
controlled more than than 25 per cent of the French legislative
body. The Communist backing of the rebellion was openly admitted by the Communists themselves. The January, 1956 issue of
Liberté, the "Clandestine Organ of the Communist Party of Algeria," expounded: "It is no sensational revelation that from the
first days of the insurrection the Communists of the Aurès and of
the south of Constantine engaged in the armed combat which
since the beginning has taken in that region the character of a
great popular battle of the masses. Many of them have fallen
gloriously on the field of honor of liberation."

In the summer of 1958, France's new president, General de
Gaulle, opened new avenues toward happier solutions of the
Algerian problem, and it seemed from the onset that his endeav-
ors might lead to success. De Gaulle's referendum plan indicated
directions of operation but no decisive final steps. It seems to me
that the Algerian question can be solved to some degree when
independence in the French Commonwealth is granted to Algeria,
not unlike the economic interdependence given to the members
of the British Commonwealth. Mendes-France and his Leftist
group had been willing to consider such an offer, even to the
murderous rebels in the hills, who lack all civilized responsibility.
But the responsible European and Moslem elements in Algeria
are able to run an independent Algeria, though sooner or later,
of course, they will have to destroy those throat-slicing bandits
who refuse to accept responsible independence and prefer chaos
and murder. In the same vein, independent Algerians will have
to tell Tunisia to mind its own business and discontinue the running of arms into their country. There are many direct and diplomatic actions which an independent Algeria can take without being denounced as promoting colonialism or imperialism.

In an Arab North African republic controlled by Nasser, the
Moslems would disregard the interests, if not the lives, of the one

million Frenchmen who were born and raised in Algeria, as were their parents, who have contributed greatly to Algeria's economic and social improvement, and who have rights there that are as well founded as those of the Moslems. In the fair election of 1958, the responsible people of all faiths, creeds, and races in Algeria voted overwhelmingly for de Gaulle and his new France and, at least by implication, for a continuing relationship with France.

It seems to me that there is no solution to the Algerian problem which can do justice to all. Of course we could say to Moscow, "Stop it—or else!" And we could say to Cairo, "Stop it—or else!" But it is debatable whether this would still be of any great help now that the fire has been ignited and is burning, perhaps out of control. Thanks to the organizing skill of Soviet-directed saboteurs, we Americans, who have strategic air bases on either side of Algeria, must watch with apprehension while the Soviet Union, with its satellites and Egypt free to aid, stirs up and abets terrorism in Algeria.

Perhaps we must embrace a "solution" which will not satisfy all concerned, perhaps not even either side, but which our security requires. That there is a chance for us to arbitrate and negotiate somewhere between the conflicting sides was shown by the patient and shrewd way in which the State Department's trouble-shooting Robert Murphy succeeded in extinguishing the fire, flaming up on the Tunisian border of Algeria, which the French military had ignited in 1958. To offer its "good offices" between the French and the Arabs seems a task worth the while of our foreign policy, although de Gaulle is not in favor of "middle men." Too much is at stake on both sides—the Arab as well as the French—to throw our lot lightheartedly to one and lose the other. While we surely cannot sacrifice the French interest, neither must we antagonize the Arabs, who could offset the whole Western defense set-up, both geographically and economically, if they become our enemies. The dilemma cannot be solved along the simplistic pattern of "colonialism" or "anti-colonialism." Here is a conflict between two groups, with the balance of injustice shifting uneasily between both, the appeasement of which is vital to our security interest. As of this writing, the world looks to de Gaulle, twice savior of France, to solve the Algerian dilemma.

FRENCH MOROCCO

Morocco is different from other North African countries. It was a protectorate of France, not a part of France, as is Algeria, or a territory of France, as was Tunisia. It differs from them in other ways, too. A chunk of land on the Mediterranean and the Atlantic, with its northern point aimed at Spain like a dagger, it has a population of identifiable breeds and interests, leaders with a mass following, and a culture all its own. The Communists are here, too, stirring up trouble, but to date, despite a few assassinations which they instigated, they have made little obvious headway. Morocco is also different in that a solution of its difficult political problems is in sight.

Long before the French came, Morocco had many remarkable and colorful leaders. Marrakech, the fabulous Baghdad of northwestern Africa, was erected by Yusuf ibn-Tashfin, a builder, fighter, and lawmaker. The workers who constructed the great city of Marrakech were accustomed to see him take off his coat and work side by side with them in shirtsleeves to show Allah his humility. But he was also inclined to fits of temper; when the laborers building the walls were working too slowly, he broke the arms and legs of these Christian slaves by throwing them off the walls. Toward the end of the eleventh century, when the Christians were pressing hard against the Moslem state in Spain, he marched north and defeated the Christian armies of Alfonso VI. This was in 1086. To prove his victory to the folks back home, he sent them the heads of more than forty thousand enemies. Some of this old-time roughness still seems to remain in the character of the Moroccan.

Another fabled leader was Ismail, the brother of Rashid II. Although legend has it that there were more than five thousand women in his harem, the truth of the matter is that he had only about five hundred, representing every race. In a letter to Louis

XIV of France, the Sun King, he asked that the Princess de Coti be sent to his harem and was quite puzzled when this flattering invitation was not accepted as a great honor. That he had more than seven hundred sons old and able enough to ride a horse was his favorite boast. The number of girl children did not count.

After a series of governmental changes and fights over succession to the throne during the first part of the twentieth century, Morocco had become the scene of almost complete chaos. Finally, Marshal Lyautey signed an agreement with the sultan whereby the French guaranteed advice and protection while the sultan would bring about necessary reforms. This was in 1912. Since then the French have more than lived up to their commitments. Where 1,000,000 acres were then planted with wheat, more than 10,000,000 acres today produce wheat for bread, without which the Moroccan cannot live. Olive trees increased from 350,000 to 21,000,000, date acreage from 5,000,000 acres to 24,000,000. Before the French, there existed no great dams in the country, while today there are seven large ones to irrigate more than 500,000 acres. The population increased from 2,500,-000 to 8,500,000 as sanitation methods were introduced by the French and as the birth rate increased with the improving living standards. In 1912, the only hospital in all of Morocco was at Fez, and it was a mental hospital whose inmates were all chained together by a metal band about their necks. Today, the French have made more than 500 hospitals and dispensaries available to the Moroccans.

Although Morocco is an important economic link between France and its associates, French records indicate that the Moroccan economy has worked at a loss; the commercial deficit—in 1951, for example, it was $217,000,000—has had to be made up almost entirely by French industry and French governmental loans. France has had its Point IV program in Morocco for years. According to Jean Basdevant, chief of the Department of Tunis and Morocco in the French Foreign Office in 1956, France advanced to Morocco approximately $70,000,000 a year for development purposes at the very low rate of 1.5 per cent interest. This had been going on since 1912, with little, if any, of the original capital ever returned or interest paid. It is well to bear these facts in mind when the soap-box orators shout against the "terrible colonial exploitation" committed by the French. In fact, French colonization was a blessing for North Africa.

The French therefore have an interest in Morocco, as is underlined with vehemence by those French pioneers who have created for themselves a place in the economy and cultural life of Morocco. They like to call themselves "Colons." More than four hundred thousand of them live, work, and raise their children in Morocco and intend to spend the rest of their lives there, if the new government will permit them.

Besides Arab Moroccans and French Colons, the population contains somewhat more than 180,000 Jews. Some of these are descendants of Jews who were driven from Spain centuries ago and who brought their advanced culture and civilization to Africa, while others descended from those who found their way in later times from areas of the eastern Mediterranean. Today, many Jews are leaving the country because of propaganda from Egypt which threatens them in the name of the Moslem League.

The Berbers of Morocco number almost three million. They are mountain men whose women do not wear veils, who have kept their ancient customs, and who love a fight. Their old enemies are the Arabs of the lowlands, against whom they have fought, on and off, for centuries.

This lack of unity between the Berbers and the Arabs—together about five million people—was brought about by the Arabs' recognition of the sultan as their religious and political head, while the Berbers recognized him only as religious leader and insisted upon their own governmental system under the alcaides of each tribe. I often heard in Morocco that the French ran the industries, the Arabs the farms, and the Jews the banking and commerce, but what the Berbers do was not explained. As you fly over the mountain areas, you wonder what they can do to eke out a living from these tiny spots of fertile land high up in the mountains. At any rate, the men of this Caucasian race, with their many blue-eyed, as well as brown-eyed, belles, are among the best soldiers in the world. Franco's Moors came from these tribes, as did the famous Goums of the French army.

The difficult situation in Morocco today is the result of a series of French "boners," the most spectacular of which was the expulsion of the sultan a few years ago. This action on the part of the French was intended to relieve the disturbances of Moroccan nationalists, but it achieved the opposite effect. Sultan Sidi Mohammed Ben Youssef had to be brought back to Morocco with full honors. Now a national hero, he gives promise of uniting the nation as it has not been united for a century. Immediately after his return, France granted Morocco its independence and, starting in Paris on February 15, 1956, steps were taken for the implementation of this decision.

The French endeavored to obtain a signed agreement with Ben Youssef providing for a limited monarchy, a so-called "independence within interdependence." In other words, independence for Morocco but reciprocal arrangements with France, particularly in the area of trade and foreign affairs. Ben Youssef has had to restrain the radical elements in his supporting Istiqlal (Independence Party), which demands complete and uncompromising severance from France, both politically and economically. Simply declaring himself king, as he did in the summer of 1957, will not solve all his problems.

At the beginning of 1957, France and Morocco concluded an agreement by which France gave Morocco a credit grant of seventeen billion francs or, at current exchange rates, $48,570,000. Two-thirds of this was a French contribution to help the newly established nation balance its extraordinary budget. One-third was a loan to semipublic corporations and public utilities. The French attached no strings to the aid. It could create a friendly fiscal and political climate in which mutual economic ties can develop between France and Morocco, which may not please some British and American interests.

Behind the political headlines a real wrestling match for economic advantage is taking place. "At the very heart of American and French difficulties lies the question of exchange controls," says Mr. William Simone, president of the American Chamber of Commerce in Morocco. "We of the Chamber of Commerce feel that punitive action taken against the French will in the long run do just as much harm to American interests in Morocco as to the French. We have been established in Morocco for many years. Some of us own apartment houses, villas, garages, warehouses. We do not feel that a belligerent approach to the problem will help us to keep them. . . . More can be accomplished through friendly relations with the French than through drastic opposition to the rules now in effect." "Not so," says Mr. Nusbaum, an American businessman in Casablanca. "The French hangover regulations make it impossible for us to do business here."

These problems were topics of conversation at the tea given in my honor at the home of General F. E. Glantzberg of the U.S. Army. The party was attended by French Minister Plenipotentiary (at that time) to the Sultan Comte de Clauzel, as well as Ben Youssef's brilliant premier at that time, Si Bekkai. It marked the first time in Morocco that a ranking Arab had visited the home of an American. He arrived at the tea in Western dress, which surprised me, having seen him pictured only in native garb. At first, his conversation in French was as formal and stiff as his artificial right leg, which is his souvenir of the Battle of Verdun in the first world war and which earned him the rank of Officer of the Legion of Honor of France for his heroic service in the French army. He warmed up to the friendliness of the group and seemed particularly pleased to be able to talk to General Glantzberg and me in the French language. When I asked him whether he preferred to be addressed by his full title or "Your Excellency" or simply as "Mister," he said: "Mister will do. After all, men make the titles, not the titles the men."

While we chatted about the New York University Institute of Physical Rehabilitation, he became particularly interested when I told him of a kitchen on display at the New York University Bellevue Medical Center designed for crippled men and women. He said that he wants to see that all Moslem women have the same opportunities as women elsewhere. This, he explained, comes easily to a Moslem because of the great love which every Moslem has for his mother.

Four key bases of the American Strategic Air Command are located in Morocco: at Nouaseur (near Casablanca), near Boulhaut, at Sidi Slimane (near Rabat), and at Benguerir in the south. Almost all of the administration, supply, and command for the Seventeenth Air Force is centered in Morocco. This air force guarantees the use of the Mediterranean to our ships in time of war, while in peace, it forms a vital link with the many American air bases which discourage the Soviet Union from brutal attacks upon our cities.

We have a big stake in Morocco. We can do business with the French, the Moroccans, or both. We can, however, stay there only with the greatest difficulty if bases are surrounded by the chaos and violence of civil war and terror. It is imperative for us to counteract these situations in Morocco. The political tightrope walking between France and Morocco is extremely difficult at times, but, fortunately, our military and diplomatic representatives in Rabat are masters in this art. They understand that we must not offend France while remaining friends of Morocco. "We especially appreciate the United States' giving up its extraterritorial rights in Morocco," Premier Si Bekkai told me. "This may not seem to be a big thing in fact, but it is a great encouragement to us and an indication of your sincere friendship. You know, Morocco was the first country to recognize the United States of America."

As I see it, Si Bekkai and Ben Youssef will be able, under the right circumstances, to do for their people what Kemal Atatürk did for Turkey. It won't be done overnight, but it is a bright hope of the future, assuming that Communist agitators, employing the latest techniques from the Soviet sabotage schools, are not able to gain strength in Moroccan life. Though Si Bekkai has since been relieved of his duties as premier, it would be a tragic loss if his guidance were entirely lost to Morocco.

SPANISH MOROCCO

A week before independence was granted to Morocco, I flew up the coast from Rabat and over to Tetuán, the capital of what was then Spanish Morocco. It had been Spanish since shortly after the death of Queen Isabella, when Spain needed a foothold on the coast of North Africa, across the strait from Spain, to protect itself from invasion. I was particularly anxious to go to Tetuán to talk with the Spanish high commissioner, Lieutenant General Raphael Garcia Valino.

It was arranged for me to see General Valino at his headquarters at nine o'clock that night. Meanwhile, I had an opportunity to drive around the countryside and see how barren the country really is. Despite all the efforts of the Spanish to improve conditions in Spanish Morocco, it is still a very poor chunk of terrain for growing anything. The Spaniards have planted hundreds of thousands of fir trees on some of the hillsides, both to halt erosion and to serve as a future source of revenue, but only the barest of fertile ground is available in what little lowland there is. Spanish Morocco is an economic expense to Spain. When Morocco was partitioned in 1912, Spain got the short end of the stick. The French got much better land.

When I was finally presented to Valino, he proved true to my expectations—a brisk, clear-thinking, concise executive. No fumbling around with words, no confusing labyrinth of sideline thoughts; straight to the issue, straight to the solution. He was one of those strong, unruffled Spanish types whom Franco picks to handle a difficult job.

I wanted to hear his views on French and Spanish Morocco after I had heard, in Madrid, a number of top business and industrial leaders complain that France had always acted in Morocco without consulting the Spanish. I asked General Valino what the position of Spain would be concerning Spanish Morocco if the French were to give complete freedom to French Morocco. His answer was direct and unequivocal. The Spanish would give complete freedom to Spanish Morocco if the French gave complete freedom to French Morocco. The Spanish would favor the union of the two parts of Morocco into a single unit under a single sultan. This independence, however, had to be completely clear and complete, not an independence with French strings. If the French were to retain economic and political controls in French Morocco, that would not be considered as complete independence by the Spanish. In such a situation, they would proceed with their plans of gradual evolution in Spanish Morocco.

Actually, it was the feeling of General Valino that the Moroccans were not yet ready for complete independence. However, were it granted by the French, the Spanish would be disinclined to oppose the desires of the Moors in Spanish Morocco. "We Spanish know the Moors, and like them. We are grateful for the great military help which the soldiers from Morocco have given to Spain, and we are doing everything possible to help them to a better economic and political life." It is my estimate that although France has given French Morocco independence, complete severance of economic and securities ties is probably not desirable at this time. Therefore, the Spanish offer is likely to remain an expression of good intent.

On its part, America must watch, with extreme caution, all new developments in the North African areas. At least in the Spanish-controlled parts, order prevails. Were Spain and France to withdraw completely from North Africa, it would be difficult to prevent the Soviets from becoming indirect rulers of the land. With the decisive strategic importance of these territories to our military security by air, sea, and land, we cannot and must not let such a thing come to pass.

PART THREE

There Will Always Be a Europe

11 *Spain: Valiant Ally*

When the Germans didn't have time to arm, when the French got bogged down in disturbances and debates, and when our North African bases were handicapped by sabotage and revolt around them, we could still count on Spain. We can still count on her; our bases under construction there are secure and effective. These bases include small ones under Spanish control in addition to our four big ones, from Cadiz, near the Strait of Gibraltar, to Zaragoza in the northeast. They are serviced by a twelve-inch pipeline running from Rota to the northernmost base. Our share in the direct and indirect costs of this establishment will probably run close to a billion dollars, while the Spanish share will be many times higher. Because modern war is a combination of economic, political, and military measures, the value of this investment cannot be understood without a close look at Spain in this light.

Americans are welcome in Spain. This seems remarkable against the background of the past, in which Spain fought hard to get rid of all the foreign forces. After Franco had asked Hitler for assistance against the Communist-controlled International Brigade, he stubbornly kept his country from an alliance with Germany in the second world war. Long before that Napoleon, who had come to Spain as a friend, could be thrown out only by an uprising of the people. In the eleventh century, it was the Almoravides who arrived to help their Moslem brothers and stayed to build up the great cities of the south, Granada and Seville, before they were evicted by the Spaniards. Today, Spain wants the

United States to remain as a fellow-fighter against the common threat presented by Soviet Communism. And as is manifest today, the United States has already contributed more to Spanish progress than all the other powers which ever become came to Spain in a common military effort. The reason is that in order to build a modern airfield, you must first build usable roads to its site. You must also bring a measure of prosperity to those who are constructing it and arrive at friendly economic and social arrangements with the people of the country, as is being done, and very skillfully, by U.S. military forces.

Why are we so interested in Spain? Why are our bases there so important? For an answer, look at an outline map of Spain. The Pyrenees Mountains across the north are impassable if guarded by even a small but determined army. Only down the coast of the Mediterranean and down the coast of the Bay of Biscay can modern armies move. It is along one of these coasts that Russia may one day move its troops, just as Hannibal moved his army up the coast, across the Alps, and into Italy.

The second reason for Spain's importance to us lies in the narrow strip of water at its extreme southern tip, the Strait of Gibraltar. It is through this strait that our ships must pass to carry food, supplies, and fuel, as ships have done in every war of modern times, including World War II. If the tactical and strategic air forces of the United States can guarantee the use of the Mediterranean in the event of war, a precondition is that the land on both sides of the Strait of Gibraltar must be held by friendly powers. On the North African side, the Communists show at least some success in weakening the West with their tactic of mixing Marxist subversion and Moslem subservience, two forces as different as oil and water yet as dangerous as nitroglycerin when agitated. On the other side, the Communists' chances of confusing or upsetting Spain are, fortunately, very slim.

One cannot understand Spain today without a close look at Generalissimo Francisco Franco. More accurately, Franco and Spain represent two different faces of the same political coin. To claim that Franco does not represent the overwhelming majority of the Spanish people means only to fool ourselves. On my visit to Spain, I found the richest men as well as the poorest workers of the cities expressing their views of Franco in unambiguous terms; that is, they are for him. Popular Spanish opinion shows an indifference toward politics which recalls German attitudes immediately after the war. "We got excited about politics, and look what happened to us," Germans said then, as Spaniards say now. If you can't talk politics to a Spaniard, the reason is not that he's afraid to talk but that he doesn't care at all, after his recent personal experience. He recalls too well that political excitement led him into a civil war in which no Spanish family escaped loss of members. A soap-box orator who would promise great future improvements by a new revolution is more likely to get a punch in the nose than applause. In the Spain of today, it is popular and appreciated to build a bridge, plow a farm, paint a house, raise a child, sing a song, or kick a soccer ball, but speeches promising a quick solution to all of life's problems are as out of date as, say, Harry Hopkins' talk would be in the United States.

The Spanish lesson seems to be that the people bought hot air and got a hurricane. In the first nine months of the "republic," between 1932 and 1933, when the Communists were playing only a minor role, the Spanish legislative body, in which dreamers and talkers predominated, attempted a great reform of Spanish life by setting up new laws. Rafael Altamira y Crevea, a competent historian of Leftist tendencies, reports in his history of Spain: "The Cortez and the republican government remade the legislation in every judicial aspect of Spanish life, the preponderant tendency of these new laws being leftist. . . . The laws covered divorce and marriage, forced labor, rentals, wages, contracts, agrarian reform, religious allegiance, penal codes, recruiting and promotion of officers, income tax, defense, pacifism, public works, land recovery, hydro-electric power, etc., etc." When well-meaning but impractical men tried to change a nation by law overnight, the result was chaos and confusion, a perfect setting for the Communists to step into, which they did soon enough.

When you mention the word "democracy" to a Spaniard today, he is likely to tell you what a Barcelona shopkeeper said to me: "Democracy? That was the word shouted when the mob beat my brother to death on the road to Madrid." A more moderate Spaniard might repeat words similar to those of my exasperated political advisor in Berlin, who, after listening to Soviet General Kotakov discoursing for a half-hour about democracy, leaned forward to whisper to me a paraphrase of Madame Roland's famous cry: "O Democracy, what crimes are committed in thy name."

If we hear continuous denunciations of Franco and his regime, many of them can be traced back to open or camouflaged Communist sources. And many leading Communists the world over have a very personal grudge. The fight against Franco in the Spanish Civil War was their revolutionary post-graduate work, and they flunked its final test. Tito fought in Spain against the present Spanish government, and so did Jacques Duclos, the driving force of the Communist party in France, as did the late Klement Gottwald, president of Czechoslovakia, François Vittori, a deputy in the French Chamber, the late Georgi Dimitrov, secretary-general of the Comintern, and the late Wilhelm Zaisser, organizer of the Communist-controlled East German People's Police (which is now recognized as the Communist-controlled army of East Germany), all, of course, under assumed names. Spaniards still remember the Russian officers who arrived during the conflict and were unable to pronounce their new Spanish aliases.

Riding over to Franco's headquarters for a personal interview, I asked my interpreter, a member of the Spanish Foreign Office, many questions about Franco. "Is he a vain man?" I wanted to know. "Does he splash his chest with medals, à la Göring?" "He couldn't care less," the interpreter grinned. "Is he sensitive about his physical lack of stature, wearing high heels and other devices that small men sometimes adopt?" "No," said the interpreter, "his height does not bother him in the slightest." "Is he hard to talk to?" I ventured. "Well, that depends," said the interpreter. "If he is bored, you'll know it. But if he's interested, he will talk freely with you." "How long should I talk to him?" I asked. "Oh, you'll know," said the interpreter, "when he has had enough conversation." "Look," said I, "I'll end the conversation. How long do you think it ought to go?" "Ten or fifteen minutes would be the usual," I was told. Our conversation lasted almost two hours!

When we entered the grounds of the old-fashioned castle, we passed Moorish guards and snappy Spanish officers. Upon our arrival in the large room in which Franco waited for us, he walked around the desk and met me to shake hands. A photographer took two shots and departed immediately to release the pictures to the Spanish press. The pictures appeared on the front page of practically every paper in Spain the next day.

The first thing about Franco to impress me was his conspicuous internal calmness. Nobody is going to push this man around or get him excited. Talking with him, I came to believe the stories of his encounters with Hitler. When the irresistible Nazi armies were at the border of Spain on the other side of the Pyrenees, der Führer demanded that Spain join the Germans in their war, but Franco merely answered "No." His answer remained the same serene, laconic "No" when Hitler wanted to march down through Spain in order to deny Allied access to the Mediterranean. According to reports, Hitler stalked up and down in front of Franco, pleaded with him, and finally ended up screaming threats at him. Franco's answer remained a quiet "No." Franco's calm is worth a great deal.

Franco and I first chatted a bit about fishing and discovered that he prefers deep-sea fishing, while I prefer trout fishing. Then we discussed his early days as a captain in North Africa, where he had introduced, with his horse cavalry, what we now call "the war of movement," as opposed to the old-fashioned method of fixed positions. Finally, we got around to the subject of France, Spain, and North Africa. "It looks like an impossible position down in North Africa, doesn't it?" I queried. Franco's smiling answer was: "It is difficult, but every problem can be solved. You must remember that the Arabs are suspicious of all foreigners and nonbelievers. Final solutions in North Africa must be worked out through the Arabs with the joint co-operation of France and Spain."

Franco believes that strong Arab leaders who are good should be backed and aided by both Spain and France. He never approved of, nor was he ever asked in advance about, the expulsion of the Sultan of French Morocco. Generalissimo Franco has deep respect for the Moroccans and the so-called Moors, whose ways he knows intimately. "They are mountain men," he said, "and mighty good soldiers. In their eyes, city men and the men who live on the lowlands are softies."

Changing subjects, I asked the Spanish chief of state why he wanted to join the United Nations after all the insults piled upon him and his government in the past by members of that organization. "We are happy to be a member now," said Franco, "and our admittance is a good way of righting past wrongs. Spain, as well as all other nations, has interrelated mutual obligations." His point of view seems to be that Spain is interested in bilateral agreements with the United States, for instance, and that these agreements are entirely adequate for the present and the future. Through such agreements, the endless debate and recriminations which might result from a suggestion that Spain, at this date, be brought into the North Atlantic Treaty Organization can be avoided.

After long discussion of various subjects, I asked Generalissimo Franco, "What happens to Spain when something happens to you? What, for example, will happen if and when you decide to spend all of your remaining years fishing? You know, we in the United States have a strong leader. When he had a heart attack, the people were so scared that the value of stocks on our New York Stock Exchange dropped fourteen billion dollars." "It is all arranged by law," said Franco. "The change will be very smooth and entirely legal. It was too bad about your great President Eisenhower, but even in his case, those stocks did gradually go back up, didn't they?" We laughed, shook hands, and I departed. His may be a dictator's democracy, but it is a reassuring state in which to have our American air bases.

The question remains whether Spain could be held if and when Soviet armies come down across Germany and France to the Pyrennes. I found nothing to permit a doubt that it can be held. Franco's army of twenty-two divisions will fight, as will the people of Spain. The Spanish soldiers are good men and are well

trained, but they lack heavy equipment. They need heavy artillery and modern communications. Many of their present weapons
were brought to Spain by the Russians during the Spanish Civil
War, and a few German 88's are still usable. Protected by an
army which will fight—and the Spaniards have some good mountain divisions—the Pyrennes are impassable for a modern enemy,
except through the narrow passages on either coast. One passage
is not much more than twelve miles wide, the other one seven
miles. These passages, used for centuries by invading armies on
their way north and south, can be completely blocked by a modern army using howitzers and tactical air support. They can be
made completely useless to the enemy if we decide to use atomic
weapons, warheads fired from howitzers or bombs dropped by
planes.

Recently, there have been sweeping changes in Spain's social
system. The big landowners who used to live in the cities without
visiting their farms, which were run by badly underpaid tenant farmers until a generation ago, have become a thing of the
past. Since 1932, land taxes on large holdings have increased by
more than 500 per cent. The usual arrangement between owner
and tenant farmer today resembles the model seen in the United
States. If the Spanish landowner pays taxes, fertilizes the land,
and supplies equipment, the tenant farmer shares the crops on a
fifty-fifty basis. If the owner pays the taxes only, the farmer usually pays the owner 25 to 30 per cent of his earnings from the
sale of crops. Land which is not cultivated is subject to confisca-
tion by the government at the lowest evaluation, which is "dry
land." The government then includes these lands in its plan for
irrigation and sells the land to those farmers who desire to buy it.

In the light of Spain's very poor fertility, such moves mean
progress. What is lacking most is water, despite Spain's many
streams. A fairly good "dry" farm produces considerably less
than one thousand pounds of wheat per acre, but this production
can be tripled with the introduction of irrigation. Our foreign-
policy experts should heed the fact that Spain needs outside help
for the development of hydro-electric energy and for the irrigation of "dry" farms.

Great poverty also prevails among Spain's city dwellers. The workers are poorly paid, and their low wages result from the lack of productivity. Not only is Spain's land poor, but her industry is backward and she still suffers from the severe wounds of the civil war and from the privations of the last world war. Yet an authoritarian increase of wage rates would hardly improve the conditions of the working class. If, overnight, all salaries in Spain were doubled under her free economy, the next day, all prices of goods would also be doubled, as was concisely explained to me by Spanish Minister of Commerce Manuel Arburua: "We are interested in improving the real wages of the working man and not in propaganda tricks which lead to nowhere. The real wages of labor can only be measured in terms of what the wages will buy." True to Arburua's statement to me, wages which had been raised 40 per cent in 1956 had lost their advantage by 1958.

Can and will Spain work with France to solve the North African problems? I had a long conference with the minister of foreign affairs. He speaks French perfectly and knows the French better than some of them know themselves. "To be strong and successful in foreign affairs," says this friend of France, "you must rule yourself. Otherwise, it is almost impossible to rule others. That is the trouble with France today. Their government and their direction of foreign affairs change so quickly and have such transient authority that the French colonial empire has come close to disintegration. The Communists, of course, are instigating trouble in all areas of tension, both in France and in North Africa." The accuracy of his appraisal has since been shown by the French vote to end the Fourth Republic.

If there are any Communists remaining in Spain (and it is estimated that there are some), they are very quiet. They need not keep their views to themselves, but they cannot publicize them over radio stations or through newspapers or through town-hall meetings, nor can they scribble insults against the United States on walls or paint them on buildings, as is done by a small Communist minority along the coast of the French Riviera.

The personality of U.S. Ambassador John Lodge may also have something to do with this happy lack of anti-Americanism in Spain, for he is one of our most popular envoys abroad. I could gauge his popularity when I was sitting in the waiting room, along with many others, to see Spanish Minister of Foreign Affairs, Alberto Martin Artajo. When Mr. Lodge appeared after his conference with Artajo, he was buttonholed by two Spanish gentlemen who were anxious to make certain business contacts in the United States. Lodge stopped, talked with them sympathetically, and gave them the information they wanted. As he turned away, he was approached by an American, an engineer who was building some of our air bases in Spain. He had a complaint against a minor official. Lodge listened to his technicalities, explained the situation, and sent the engineer away, completely satisfied. As the Ambassador walked across the room, he saw an old Spanish friend, put his arm around him, and consoled him over the loss of his wife. John Lodge represents America and our interests in Spain very ably. As I see it, we must befriend and strengthen our valiant ally by military, political, and economic means. Whether we like Spain's internal order or not, we profit by its achievements, its partnership, on which we can depend, its strength, and its stability.

12 France: Strength out of Confusion

"I love Paris in the springtime." These words to a popular song weren't yet written when I was very young, or the song would have been my favorite even then as it is now. After my graduation from New York University, I went to Paris and studied at the Sorbonne. Much later, I fought in the second world war side by side with French troops, and toward the end of the war, the Army put me in charge of civil affairs in Cherbourg, then Paris. I was there in the days of liberation and have been there often since.

Old acquaintance and deep affection tie me to France, but love must not blind us to the realities. Today, France, as far as it concerns the interests of America, poses military rather than sentimental problems. We have a big investment in France in the Cold War, which could very quickly turn into a hot war if we bungle.

Many Americans have been puzzled and disturbed by the words and actions of postwar France. They have seen a French policy which, with its wavering weakness, has hardly deserved that name and an endless sequence of cabinets which have come and gone as through a revolving door. "France used to be a great nation, but now it's a fourth-rate power," I have heard a diplomat in Washington assert, and he was echoed by an American general: "We might as well write off the French as a military loss and concentrate on our best asset, the West Germans." And many an American traveler returns with a bitter sigh: "The French don't like us, so why don't we stay home and leave them to their own devices?"

These views were expressed before de Gaulle and his new Fifth Republic. Furthermore, they were based on misinformation. Seen from the inside, France is strong, and the French people are a great people. What was shamefully weak was France's national central government. Unfortunately, it was with this central government that we had to deal in international intercourse; were this not so, we could agree with the French: the less central government, the better. This attitude recalls what Thomas Paine said in 1776: "Society in every state is a blessing but government, even in its best state, is but a necessary evil, in its worst state an intolerable one." Finally, even the French were driven to a rejection of their weak Fourth Republic and into the arms of de Gaulle's strong Fifth Republic.

If you take a plane from Madrid and fly across the Pyrenees, you see a rather striking aspect of what makes France a great power. Below you spread some of the 213,000 square miles of France, 46 per cent of them green with crops, another 30 per cent with grasslands, meadows, and pastures, and 19 per cent with well-kept forests. This leaves hardly any room for wasteland. In fact, by comparison, the triangle of usable land in Russia, running north from the Black Sea, seems marginal and unproductive.

France produces all of the food it needs and could double food production if it wanted to. But this is not feasible, since French farmers resist any changes in their way of life, including the introduction of tractors and wholesale farm methods. Yet in his own way, the French farmer is still one of the greatest farmers of the world.

Twenty-six thousand miles of railroad in France transport French farm products, travelers, and the products of the nation's busy industry, whose output today is 75 per cent higher than ever before in history. These railroads, in addition to highways based on the old Roman roads, can be a lifesaver for our military supply system in Europe in the event of war. General Patton, of happy memory, knew this when he told his provost marshal: "Use the Roman highways across France. They are built deep and won't break down under pressure."

It may well be that in the next few years, some Frenchmen will overcome their reluctance and embrace more modern economic methods on their farms, in their retail trade, and in their industries. A few might even stoop down to forego a little joy of life and work a little harder instead.

Normally, the Frenchman cares particularly little about foreign affairs. The world outside his country does not interest him; you find fewer people in France who speak foreign languages than in any other major country of Europe. Another French characteristic is the reluctance to pay taxes. The Frenchman avoids tax-paying completely, whomever he may vote for. Before de Gaulle, 71.4 per cent of his taxes were indirect or hidden taxes. Even if he saw them, he would not have paid them, and the central government had plenty of difficulty collecting the 28.6 per cent of the tax which was direct. This situation seems rather different from that in America, where comparatively patient and obedient citizens pay 75.6 per cent of their taxes directly and only 24.4 per cent indirectly.

The central government of France functions only in the form of the perennial and ubiquitous civil service; its members run almost everything in the land, from social security to railroads and postal services, and the French people accept them without protest. The civil service presents the French element of continuity in public affairs against a background of changing political leadership. Whether governments promise to raise additional taxes or additional troops, the French people just look the other way and refuse to listen, let alone back them up. Against this attitude, there was no constitutional corrective under the Fourth Republic. In fact, the French people had deliberately written their constitution in such a way that it prevented the executive branch of the central government from ever attaining strength or even the capability of becoming strong. They recalled too well some of their sad experiences with powerful central executives—shades, above all, of Napoleon! Four times in the past two hundred years have the French seen themselves compelled to overthrow their national government by force because it had become too strong. "The man on horseback" is no joke to a Frenchman. The only terms under which the unwieldy constitution and the feeble basis of the central government of the Fourth Republic could possibly be changed had to be a great national emergency, a war or a revolution.

In 1958, France was ripe for revolution, but the French seem almost too smart to go through a revolution and almost too sophisticated to fight a war personally. The French people are not weak if you talk, say, with Madame Antoinette, the fishmonger, in Marseilles, or with Madame "Bobo" in her fashionable salon in Paris; in fact, they never had it so good. To find out about France's tremendous industrial strengthening since the war, look at the brand new taxis in Paris which have replaced the old ramshackle jobs; observe the new French fastest-in-the-world streamline trains; share the ample lunch of a French worker. The people would like to have it stay that way, preferably without a strong central government but of necessity with the powerful new constitution of the Fifth Republic.

What France does have with no uncertainty is strategic land, which is an important part of modern warfare. General Maxwell Taylor's Pentagon plans for the use of guided missiles require suitable sites from which to launch them. Of course, aircraft carriers help, but in war, there is no substitute for real estate.

A second great asset of French strength is its industry. No nation can be written off as weak that can produce in one year more than 57,000,000 tons of coal, 42,000,000,000 kilowatt-hours of electric power, and more than 13,000,000 tons of steel. Nor is a nation weak that can produce, as the French are producing, more than 500,000 automobiles a year.

There remains the problem of the French people themselves, who admittedly enjoy life rather than slave to acquire additional material wealth. But when the pressure is on, they are capable of incredible energy and determination, as was amply demonstrated during the German occupation of France during the last war.

If many Americans tend to underestimate the potential vigor of the French today, they may have second thoughts when they muse over a little story which my French friends told me. They had been in Paris under the Nazi occupation, when the Germans ran the great automobile factories of Renault and Citröen. At the time, Allied planes flew over Paris in bright daylight to bomb these plants. When they showed up, my friends and many other Parisians would run into the streets to cheer the American and British bombers, without fear of the Nazi guards and German soldiers nearby. When an Allied plane was shot down by German anti-aircraft guns, the populace would moan loudly, yet when white parachutes would open in the air—the sign that no Allied airmen had been killed—they would applaud. On one such day, a German major and his two aides stood close to my friends, who heard him complain: "*Ach!* What can you do with these people? We treat them correctly, we give them work in the factories, we are as nice to them as can be, but when our enemies come to destroy their factories, they are happy." The answer, my friends said, though nobody gave it, would have been to continue making friends with the French and never underestimate them. This piece of advice also goes for our relations with the French these days.

Yet in turn, the French people seem rather disinclined nowadays to continue being friends of ours. Although it happened not so long ago—in the second world war, that is—it seems like a very distant past that the President of the United States, in an address to the French people, asserted: "No two nations exist which are more united by historic and mutually friendly ties than the people of France and the United States." Neither this nor any of the many similar statements, as they resounded in and after the war, would be accepted and approved in France today. If a new General Pershing would say again, "Lafayette, we are here," the French would merely respond with cat calls.

If the British showed an anti-American temper after Suez because they felt let down by our action, the French, rather than be disappointed, saw in it a reaffirmation of their more ancient and cynical ideas about what to expect from us. Most French men and women tend to be cynics when it comes to public life; they have long maintained that despite international organizations, each nation should take recourse to those actions which seem best for itself. If the French Communists had long been claiming that

the Americans were no better than the Russians and that they
would take advantage of the French, particularly in the Middle
East oil situation, just as the Russians might take advantage of
the French elsewhere in the world, the French people saw this
confirmed by our actions during the Suez crisis.

I heard this again and again when I visited some of my old
haunts and some new places, talking with our ambassador, with
French generals, with old friends of my school days in Paris, as
well as with waiters, barbers, and others, in short, a fairly good
cross-section of French opinion. Before arriving in Paris, I read
an article in the January 9, 1957 issue of a leading paper of
Paris, *Le Figaro,* which very clearly explained the anti-American
feeling in France and, to some extent, that in England. "I have
been hearing and still hear every day what has been said in France
for some time—to be precise, since the beginning of the Suez
crisis," the newspaper editor wrote. "I must tell you that now it
is becoming serious. The adversaries of NATO would not so
noisily proclaim in writing that the life of the Atlantic Pact is
practically over if they did not feel their chances growing. The
Franco-American friendship is in danger."

The danger, as I see it, would be that the Soviet Union, if it
attacked the West, would meet little resistance from the French.
Of course, our troops in Germany would fight, as would a limited
number of British troops and a few French soldiers. But with the
main French army, 400,000 strong, busy in Algerian warfare,
the French civilians called to the arms would have little emotional
cause to do battle.

As I was told by my friends of the French army, this situation
was brought to a head by Suez. A general known for his judgment,
his friendship with the United States, and his ability to appraise
situations exclaimed: "Frank, *mon ami,* the U.S. action concerning the Suez was a tragedy. If you had let us fight, within forty-
eight hours the problem of the Suez could have been solved."
He continued: "Over the attack on the Suez, the French were
united from top to bottom as they have not been united in modern
times. It was recognized by all that the only possible way to solve
the Algerian question and to put an end to the horrible atrocities

was to bring about the fall of Egypt's Nasser and his group of followers, who are guiding and supporting the Algerian rebels. The position of the Soviet Union, which encourages the Algerian rebels and supports the Egyptian government, which, in turn, supports the rebels, does not seem much worse to the average Frenchmen than the stand of the United States. You emulated the United Nations in condemning France, Britain, and Israel and played a leading part in stopping the war before anything was accomplished." Another French general said: "Immediately after the Suez incident, the Soviet Union had a wonderful opportunity to break up our North Atlantic Treaty Organization completely. Fortunately, they were too busy with internal affairs and with the Hungarian rebellion to follow up their advantage."

I was interested in getting the opinion on this subject of the American Ambassador to France, the competent Amory Houghton. "The French people and the American people have so much in common," he said, "that this present feeling will not last. Time is a great healer. However, as you say, right now would not be a good time to run a popularity contest."

Today, however, it's going to take more than diplomacy to heal the wound caused by our action over the Suez. Witness a waiter in a restaurant on the Place Voltaire. I was accompanied by a member of a French family with whom I had lived back in 1929, '30, and '31 when I studied in Paris. The Place Voltaire, I suppose, would be considered a poor part of town if anybody could classify Frenchmen or a section of Paris according to such clear-cut social terms. An aristocratic part of Paris a century ago, it is now the heart of a working-class district in which the Communists are particularly active. The waiter recommended *coq au vin,* and when I had enjoyed the dish, I said to him: "You made a good choice for me. This *coq au vin* is delicious. That chicken was born to be cooked in wine." "And the green beans?" he asked. "I've never tasted beans like them," I said. "What did you add?' "Oh," he said, "the recipe is a secret, but you are a gourmet." It didn't take much conversation like this before he opened up. "I like New York," he told me. "I used to work on the *Liberté.* The captain, he is now retired. I left the

ship because I want to stay here with my family instead of being
on the sea all the time. Your French is excellent, Monsieur. I
like you Americans, but why did you forsake us over Suez?"

Down near the Bastille, a small group of people were gathered.
I walked over and listened to the conversation. The speaker was
obviously a Communist. He was talking to the crowd about Algeria. "Let us get out of Algeria!" he shouted. "We Frenchmen
are being killed there. Half a million soldiers are draining our
taxes because they're down there fighting a stupid war for the
imperialists. In the end, only America will gain." "What's America got to do with this?" heckled someone from the crowd. "Oh,
so you don't know!" the Communist shouted. "Don't you read
the newspapers? Didn't the Americans stop us or, rather, stop
you from the aggression against Egypt? You know that Egypt
and Algieria are friends. Both fight against the imperialists for
their freedom." "What's Russia doing?" someone yelled. "Oh,"
said the Communist, "what difference is there between the Soviet
Union and the imperialists in America? We are Frenchmen. Let
us be neutral and mind our own business. The Suez must prove
to you that the Soviets stick by their friends, while the Americans
run out on their friends. Let them fight their own battles, and
let us be neutral between Russia and America for the good of
the ordinary working Frenchman."

The Communist was echoed by a French barber talking to a
French customer in the chair next to mine. "What's the matter
with this American Senator Kennedy? He attacks us for Algeria.
Why doesn't he attack himself for supporting Israel? We have
been in North Africa longer than Israel has been in Palestine.
Doesn't he know any better? Is he a fool? Doesn't he know Algiers is a part of France? What would he say if the state of Ala-
bama wanted to secede from the United States? What did the
United States do when a number of Southern states tried to set
up a free republic? Now he gives us advice, after Suez. If this is
the best advice they give, maybe they'd better give no advice.
Je m'en fiche of the whole affair."

But, happily, I happened to walk behind a group of French
women in the Tuileries Gardens, through the splendid exhibit of

art owned and brought to France by Robert Lehman. The women were obviously as impressed as I was by its magnificent display and good taste. *"Eh bien,"* said one matron, "even after Suez, perhaps we have something in common with the Americans."

Yet among the dozens of French comments from people in high and humble positions, from friends and those not so friendly, ranging from outright condemnation of the United States to a tolerant understanding of our position, which I have heard, every single one stressed that the action of the United States at the time of the Suez crisis was an unsympathetic, unfriendly action and an unfortunate rejection of our century-old friendship.

Danger of revolution, the return of de Gaulle, elections, and a new constitution have stolen the recent headlines, but the Suez affair still sharpens the strong neutralist sentiment which runs throughout France, although it conflicts with a widespread awareness that the French need the United States. It is up to us to underline this second tendency and overcome the first. To do this is of paramount importance for our own sake. Whatever French domestic policies may look like, they concern us only if they affect the French military strength. The military, political, and economic condition of France can still be one of our best assets abroad if it is backed by our own power. While we are looking for allies abroad, it's all well and good for us to win, say, Ecuador, Peru, or Tanganyika, but France is worth fighting for. To lose France would be disastrous. The whole structure of NATO, with headquarters in Paris, would come down like an axed tree. Without France on our side, Europe would be lost to Communism. Despite all its annoying and sometimes shocking attitudes and actions, France must remain our ally, and we must do everything in our power to keep it that way. Out of a politically confused France is emerging a new nation of political, economic, and military greatness.

13 A New France: From Confusion to De Gaulle

I liked Charles André Joseph Marie de Gaulle the very first time I met him. In 1944, this was an unusual reaction for an American, and it goes to show that I am a non-conformist, for all of those who conformed to Roosevelt's desires and the desires of our State Department at that time disliked de Gaulle as a matter of principle.

It was shortly after the landings in Normandy that I met General de Gaulle. I was military governor of Cherbourg at the time, and as *chèf des affaires civiles,* I had a detachment of expert British and American officers and enlisted men. We were very busy, for the city had just been captured. Water mains were broken, disease was threatening, the food supply was low, the police force was disorganized, and so forth.

We were hard at work to establish normal conditions again when I received a surprising bit of information, along with an invitation. The information was that de Gaulle, who had been granted provisional recognition to head a government in France, had arrived. A reception was to be held for him that afternoon, but the commander of U.S. troops in the port of Cherbourg had refused to attend the reception, as had the American admiral who was in charge of clearing the harbor of mines in order to make it usable. The local representative of de Gaulle was rather desperate, since nobody was available to represent the United States or, for that matter, Britain either. But since I've never yet turned down an invitation for good champagne and good companionship, my deputy, British Colonel R. L. H. Nunn, and

I told him that we'd be delighted to meet the General. Nunn and I walked to the reception, which was to be held at the ancient Prefecture Maritime. As we approached the cobbled courtyard, French sailors lined up on either side and presented arms while drums rolled and cannons fired. Surprised by all this pomp, I noticed that Colonel Nunn kept looking over his shoulder as we passed through the honor guard. Then he remarked, with a twinkle in his eye: "There must be somebody really important in back of us because they couldn't possibly go through all of these honors just for two lieutenant colonels."

We went inside, shook hands with de Gaulle, a tall, rather austere, but friendly giant, and exchanged pleasantries with him for a few minutes. I recall that he expressed his great appreciation for what the people of the United States were doing for France; he mentioned especially the repair of one of the French battleships in the Philadelphia shipyards.

My next encounter with General de Gaulle was in Paris, where I was again in charge of civil affairs for the British, Americans, and, to some extent, the French Allies until the regular French government could take over. We Americans were usually opposing de Gaulle, belittling his efforts, and, it seemed to me, trying to make him fail in his efforts to secure control of France and to bring about healthy changes in the French government. There was much talk in those days that he was a Rightist, or that he was a Leftist, that he was a dictator, that he was politically unwise, that he was this, that, or the other thing. To call him "the man who thought he was Joan of Arc" was only one of the more harmless jokes, at de Gaulle's expense, about which Roosevelt and Churchill used to chuckle and which American officials found quite hilarious. We knew well that Roosevelt had gone out of his way to snub the French leader when he failed to call on him in Paris on the way back from Teheran after he had paid a well-publicized official call on King Sa'ud of Saudi Arabia, presented him with a wheel chair, and received a goat in return. What was worse, we knew that de Gaulle was deeply hurt by this snub.

Whatever the occasion, de Gaulle, his representatives, and his provisional government were ignored by our leaders. For instance, I brought crates of invasion francs printed in America for use by our occupation troops. Since at the time the French currency issued by the Vichy government was also circulating, de Gaulle asked us for a statement of policy on the nature of this money, which would have implied an open condemnation of the Vichy government. But I could not give out, or get any American authority to give out, such a statement. When the local representative of the Bank of France, with his understandable doubts about this American-French currency which nobody seemed to back, visited me, I could persuade him of its standing only by makeshift explanations. Even on such matters as this, our government refused to help or co-operate with de Gaulle.

When after our successful work in Cherbourg we went with the liberating troops into Paris, I had orders from the chief of civil affairs of the First Army to stand by without action, neither to purify water nor to reorganize the police nor to distribute food, in short, not to assist in bringing life to the city of Paris. No reasons for such orders were given. Paris was in bad shape then, with riots in the streets, with the twenty-two thousand city police on strike, and with the food ration down to nine hundred calories per day, a starvation level. There was no heat, light, or power; women were tearing up the wooden pavement to use it as fuel for cooking. When I arrived, by means of a breakthrough in the German lines, with 130 truckloads of food and almost 500 British and American military-government experts, I was in no mood for sitting around while de Gaulle and his supporters underwent the difficult and unfair test of trying to discover whether they could establish order and be accepted by the French. I selected a headquarters at Place Vendome for the central group, took over the Hotel Loti for my officers, billeted the enlisted men in the Hotel Normandy, and sent a team of military-government experts out to each of the twenty boroughs of Paris. After one passive day, which was enough to impress upon me the rapid deterioration of the situation, I got in touch with de Gaulle by way of Colonel La Rocque, my brilliant French liaison officer (who is now a member of the Supreme Court of France), to let him know what my orders were and to ask whether he wanted my co-operation. Word came back from General Koenig, de Gaulle's right-hand man at the time, that "Howley and his gang should please pitch in as they did in Cherbourg and help us." We were happy to be given the green light and proceeded accordingly, and our work was gradually taken over and accomplished by the legitimate de Gaulle officials until law and order were re-established.

De Gaulle showed great political courage in the ways in which he performed that job. One particular incident impressed me deeply. With our units in every borough of the city, we were in a good position to observe the local goings-on, and we soon discovered that the Communists had begun, surreptitiously, to control Paris. After the Allied conquest of Paris, most of the resistance fighters of the FFI (the Free Forces of the Interior) had disbanded, except for the hard core of its members under Communist orders. These Communists moved now into each borough, forcibly installed their representatives as mayors, and put their members, as armed guards, at each borough hall. They were running mock courts, penalizing people, throwing charges here and there, and often ordering executions. Since this wasn't justice as we knew it, a rather complete report was prepared, documented, and sent to General Eisenhower's headquarters (SHAEF). The reports were studied, and information was sent to de Gaulle, probably by his ambassador at large, François Coulé. De Gaulle called a special meeting of his cabinet, told them the facts, and asked them whether or not he should order that all arms be turned in and FFI jurisdiction abolished.

In my report, I had quoted the Paris prefect of police who had told me that if he received orders to disband and disarm these illegal gangs, he would need rifles for his policemen, who were equipped only with pistols. Now pistols carried by Paris police weren't very useful against automatic machine guns and other high-powered weapons, which the Communists had, somehow or other, "liberated" from captured German supplies. But my request for rifles for the Paris police was turned down. All of this was known to de Gaulle, and his cabinet members advised him against any drastic steps against the FFI, as they were afraid of civil war. Nonetheless, de Gaulle went on the air that night and ordered the FFI to turn in its weapons and discontinue its practices. In response, some followed suit and did turn in a few of their weapons, but the others went underground, in the usual procedure of Communists when "called." No civil war followed, and after this initial success, de Gaulle was able to take a second step against the Communists. He refused to grant their demand to establish their own division-size units, commanded by FFI Communist generals, within the regular French army. The happy results of this decision were revealed years later. When the Communists opposed France's inclusion in the Marshall Plan, the French government could count upon the loyalty of its army and join us. Without de Gaulle and his courage in 1945, we would not even need to ask whether he likes or dislikes NATO because there would be no NATO now and France would be Communist.

Soon after the liberation of France, de Gaulle visited Moscow and conferred with Stalin. It has always seemed strange to me that upon his return to Paris, and for months thereafter, he was attacked as a stooge of the Communists. The conference meetings were, of course, held in secret, but one participant told me of a significant incident which occurred at the time. When Stalin proposed a toast in which he alluded to a future Communistic France working hand in hand with the Soviet Union, de Gaulle refused to drink it.

After studying de Gaulle's brilliant ideas, written before the invasion of France while he was a junior officer, and on the basis of my personal acquaintance and professional experiences in military-government operations, I consider him one of the greatest men produced by France in the last one hundred years. Today, the French people themselves have come to realize this, despite the discouraging course of events after the liberation of France. Even if he had been uncompromising, the French people came to realize in 1958 that their national inclination toward compromises would not suit all situations or times. After the war, de Gaulle wanted France to live up to its past glories, but the French people of that day preferred more bread and an end to all struggle. In 1958, they discovered that no nation can live by bread alone and that, in short, de Gaulle had been right.

During the war, the United States could see as its goal in the war only the defeat of the German Army, but de Gaulle visualized from the beginning what a vital role a rebuilt France would eventually have to play in world leadership. American policy let de Gaulle down because Franklin D. Roosevelt disliked him personally and also because certain Leftist elements in our State Department and policy-making bodies favored both a weak France and a weak Germany as equally important steps in the Communist master plan of world conquest. If they succeeded, though only for a brief moment, in Germany by applying the Morgenthau Plan and by keeping that country in a slum status, they also succeeded (though for a somewhat less brief moment) in France. Had France and Germany remained weakened long enough, Europe would have been a power vacuum which the Soviets could have taken before attacking America.

But the French people were not very anxious to keep de Gaulle at the helm of their nation's ship of state. In their postwar temper, they disliked his notions of change and power and preferred quietism, the comforts of the *status quo,* and something better on their luncheon tables than potatoes and an occasional stewed rabbit. When they left little doubt that what they desired more than anything else was rest and private well-being, de Gaulle retired to the life of a country squire.

By 1958, the French temper, rather than de Gaulle, had changed, although his former opponents claimed that he, rather than they, had matured. By this claim, those who still disliked him could at least apologize for their change of heart, since, as they admitted, "there was no choice but de Gaulle." The great change came to pass after the Chamber of Deputies had shown that it was democracy gone to seed, a legislative executive body completely paralyzed in its action. Before de Gaulle's reforms, the last step to social chaos (a chaos stimulated and encouraged by Communists wherever they are in government) had been taken. The final chaos of a civil war was avoided in the last analysis by the good sense of the French people when they recalled de Gaulle, an uncompromising man who was willing to use dictatorial methods for the benefit of his country. The insults hurled at him at the end of the last war were now swallowed by the wisecracking wits, for even Joan of Arc could not have done a better job uniting the French people in an all-out effort to save France. From professor to street cleaner, from lady to charwoman, the French people were behind Charles de Gaulle in 1958 and continue so in 1959.

As I see it, de Gaulle's job was threefold after saving France from bloody revolution. First, he had to create a central government able to make commitments and bring about actions; words and discussions are not ends in themselves but means to an end. Second, he had to settle the Algerian problem and take positive steps toward ending the shooting in Algeria until problems could be worked out under peaceful conditions. His third job was to bring France back to a respected place in the councils of democratic nations. Given the backing of the French people, and recent elections show that he has it, he can accomplish all of these things and, in so doing, perform once again a service of tremendous value to both France and the United States.

14 England: Powerhouse of Force

It was in Chicago at a meeting on the defense and foreign policy of the United States that the featured speaker proclaimed to an audience of thousands: "The British are through, all washed up, finished. They had their day, but the new day belongs to the Asian-African peoples. That's where our American future is, not in the old world of the past. Now I sympathize with the British, and we recognize our old ties, but new ties are needed by the United States. If we told the African and Asian people, 'You can't join our club,' they would form their own clubs and we would lose out on the future as well as the present. We're sorry for England, but it's a thing of the past." Unfortunately, the speaker is not alone in his views. One can hear and read them quite often in this country, where many so-called "experts" work hard, and successfully, to build up the Asian-African bloc at the expense of our traditional allies and present-day NATO partners, Great Britain in particular.

Just how dead, though, is England today? In 1588, King Philip II of Spain announced that England was dead, but when he sent his "Invincible Armada" to clean up what was left of English power, Sir Francis Drake and his outnumbered English fleet put it to rout in the Channel. I remember hearing Kaiser Wilhelm and, twenty years later, Adolf Hitler cheerfully announce the death of England, just as Napoleon had done a century before. Based only on wishful thinking, these men's announcements of England's death were premature; in fact, England has survived them all. Today, she is strong economically and militarily and is more united than ever before. Of course, the military strength of her ground troops, for example, appears less overwhelming than before when compared with that of other nations. But she has nothing to fear from a comparison with the Asian-African bloc, in whose areas we find nothing to indicate ability to fight an all-out modern war, nor is there any great industrial capability either. Our sympathy for them as human beings and our will to encourage them in their struggle to better their living conditions must not lead us to fallacious comparisons with the power of Great Britain.

If you think that England is dead, take another look. The English thrive on difficulties. In fact, they are at their best when the going is tough. Winston Churchill expressed their temperament when he referred to their conduct in World War II as "their finest hour." If this was their reaction in time of war, they are now in their finest peacetime hour in industry and trade. The astonishing revival of Great Britain is often underestimated abroad, a direct consequence of the British habit of understating things. While others glorify their ten-year plans, publicize their blueprints, and present elaborate mock-ups of their progress, the British quietly do their job, which consists in building a bigger, more powerful nation.

The best gauge, perhaps, with which to measure the power of a nation in this age is its steel-producing ability. Great Britain is well provided with coal and iron ore from which, with her industrial know-how, she produces steel for automobiles, tanks, airplanes, buildings, ships, and other essential hardware of war and peace. While in 1945 less than 9,000,000 tons of steel were produced in the British Isles, approximately 20,000,000 tons were produced in 1955 and over 23,000,000 tons in 1958. In contrast to the lack of steel-producing ability in any of the Afro-Asian nations, Britain's achievements compare only with those of the Ruhr district in Germany, with its similar output, or with Soviet Russia, whose total production may possibly approach that figure.

Witness another example. Between 1946 and 1955, Britain increased her annual production of passenger cars from 219,000 to 897,000. Production in 1955 was 72 per cent above that of 1950, with an output of 898,000 cars, 44 per cent of which were exported to other parts of the world. To expect a similar performance from the Asian-African group is tantamount to running after a moonbeam while sitting on a pot of gold.

The second new achievement to impress you in England these days, after you've dodged the terrific flow of modern cars and trucks on the streets, is the building boom. Between 1945 and 1950, only 843,106 houses were completed, while 307,274 apartments were constructed in 1956 alone. London doesn't look the same, nor does it sound the same, as of old. When I stayed at my favorite Hyde Park hotel in 1957 and 1958, I couldn't work in my room because of the noise from construction work going on all about.

The face of London has been lifted too. Building façades have been painted, shop windows overflow with merchandise, people walk with a springier stride and are better dressed. The gentlemen are again living up to their reputation of being the best-dressed men in the world, while the distaff side still seems to glory in the equally old adage that "French girls are beautiful because of their clothes, while English girls are beautiful despite their clothes."

Britain's exports are stepping up and are encouraged by the government. Although one-fourth of the entire wealth of Great Britain was destroyed during the war, when much of the shipping of the Commonwealth was sent to the bottom of the sea, she had recovered 20 per cent of the world's export business by 1955, despite the rising tide of West German competition, which by then held 15.5 per cent of the world market. With the many attractive English automobiles speeding along American roads and successfully competing with our own vast automobile industry, we see impressive proof of the strides that Britain is making in even the most highly competitive fields.

The English are not starving themselves to bring about this industrial progress. On the contrary, their average per capita daily food consumption is 3,130 calories, and this includes meat for muscle, as well as starches and carbohydrates for energy. The poor, emaciated native of the Upper Congo, living as he has for two thousand years, or the hoe-wielding, disease-ridden farmer of the Nile or the half-starved Chinese coolie in Communist China could never compete with the physical drive of one of the fifty million experienced, intelligent, and well-fed Britons. One-half of all the food eaten in Britain is now produced at home, while before the war, the British Isles could only produce one-third of the food requirements for the then much smaller population. Increased fertilization and increased use of machinery have made possible this advance toward self-sufficiency.

Or take the subject of electric power if you want to compare "dying" England with the new Afro-Asian nations. The latter, we hear, would arrive at an enviable state of health and vigor if only that one missing giant hydro-electric plant were built in each country—with money and skills donated by the West, of course, and notwithstanding the fact that even a new hydro-electric plant would work out only if the other social and economic developments of the country could keep pace with it, which they scarcely could. Then look at England, which ranks third in world power production after the United States and Canada. To satisfy demand, Great Britain uses 250,000,000 tons of coal each year; additional power is derived from oil, and soon more power will be furnished by a peaceful use of atomic energy. By 1962, the latter is to produce more than 15 per cent of all the energy needed to run the industries of Great Britain.

It must be admitted that Great Britain has led—and is still leading—the United States when it comes to advances in the atomic field. As much as we have achieved in this field, from atomic submarines to hydrogen bombs, it has often been based on the findings of foreign scientists who came to our shores or whose discoveries we applied in practice. Much of the scientific strength of England stems from her most impressive asset: the education of her people. While illiteracy in the world's backward areas runs from 80 per cent to more than 90 per cent, as in Egypt or India, and near 100 per cent, as in most of Africa, where some tribes communicate only by clucking the tongue, education in England is compulsory between the ages of five and fifteen, and higher education is given to ever widening circles.

A shift to atomic energy as the new basis of British strength has been occurring in the military field since shortly after Suez. In April, 1957, the British minister of defense announced a brand new policy to his people and to the world at large. As he reported, "the time has now come to revise not merely the size but the whole character of the defense plan. The Communist threat remains, but its nature has changed, and it is now evident that on both military and economic grounds, it is necessary to make a fresh appreciation of the problem and to adopt a new approach towards it." Among the startling revelations of this report was the fact that "it must be frankly recognized that there is, at present, no means of providing adequate protection for the people of this country against the consequences of an attack with nuclear weapons. . . . This makes it more than ever clear that the overriding consideration of all military planning must be to prevent war rather than to prepare for it. . . . The only existing safeguard against major aggression is the power to threaten retaliation with nuclear weapons."

In accordance with this consequential decision, Great Britain has shifted from her reliance on the army, the navy, and the air force to a concentration of her energy and money on the weapons of nuclear warfare, from guided missiles to atomic and hydrogen bombs. The momentous turn might have resulted from the lesson Great Britain learned when she suddenly stopped the Suez campaign short of all-out victory. If, British military leaders may have thought, ground troops were useless in putting out a brush fire in the Middle East, then what is the use of such ground troops altogether? As long as the Soviet Union could threaten England with nuclear destruction, England had better stop wasting its money and time on the old-fashioned ground, sea, and air forces. Until Great Britain can completely offset any Soviet threat by a counter-threat of retaliation against the Soviet Union, there is no point in fighting, with traditional arms, those minor wars which are stirred up and supported by the Soviet Union.

Whether British reasoning ran along these lines or not, Britain made a sound decision which may well enable her independently to defend herself and to prevent war against her, with or without American support. Although I am fully convinced that Great

Britain has no intention of backing out of her NATO commitments or of severing her military relationships with the United States, it is also obvious that she strives for a position from which she can protect her islands and the Commonwealth against another Russian ultimatum of the kind which might have been delivered in the Suez crisis.

In hindsight, it may seem strange that many American sympathies at the time of the Suez campaign swung away from England and France toward Egypt—and thus toward the Soviet Union —merely because they were emotionally conditioned to take the "anti-colonial" side. In America, "colonialism" has become associated with all the other bad things of the world. Public opinion seems almost united on this, from the pamphleteering by a justice of the United States Supreme Court to voices from pulpit, editorial columns, and Congress, all condemning the white man's crime. While these voices repeat their denunciations of France, Holland, Belgium, Portugal, and particularly of Great Britain, blood is flowing in the streets of Bombay, Accra, Leopoldville, and at least a dozen other spots where natives rise up against their colonial rulers.

But is colonialism—that is, each and every form of colonialism and each and every instance of colonial rule as it exists today— really that bad? If we admit many past excesses and some present ones in the name of colonialism, surely we must also admit that similar and worse crimes have been committed in the name of freedom from colonialism. And slavery, so often associated with colonialism, had been practiced by natives on their own people. To give the other side of the colonial story in fairness, we must remember that white men brought to backward areas the religion of Christ, the ambitions of energetic peoples, the administrative skills of organized minds, and the standards of morality, ethics, and sportsmanship. Given these imports to various colonies, including the early American colonies, colonialism was perhaps the best thing ever to happen to the natives.

Even modern anti-colonial mass struggles could not have been fought without native leaders trained by the colonizing powers. Mahatma Gandhi, that great Indian teacher of passive resistance, got his ideas, as a student in England, from reading Henry David Thoreau's *Walden,* with its ideas of civil disobedience to government and taxation. Krishna Menon, the Communist errand boy with the Indian delegation in the United Nations for so many years, also learned the art of politics, mainly consisting in the artful use of words, in England, where he lived and was educated in his youth. It was the same with Kwame Nkrumah and Jomo Kenyatta and all the other liberators whose ideas and inspirations came from their colonizing teachers. In most backward areas, the degree of native modernization and advancement corresponds precisely to the degree of colonial penetration. Travel along the coast of Africa, where colonizing has been most intent, and you will find modern roads, schools, and law and order as we know it. But once you advance farther inland into areas not reached by colonization, you will encounter the witch doctor, hunger, and injustice.

One can pretend that these backward areas have been held down by the colonizers only if one denies or ignores the facts. At most one may accuse colonizers of not having lifted them up fast enough, as do small groups of Western-educated natives who claim that they themselves can apply Western standards at greater speed. It will be interesting to see, during the next ten years, whether or not these backward areas, under their own native leadership, will really attain their goals of quick progress. From my observation throughout Africa, I find it doubtful. The new leaders are already meeting serious opposition from their own people. They find that their people do not want to change their old ways and work hard for the promised new world. It may well be that these backward countries, while they are now going it on their own, will go backward instead of forward and that their leaders will be confronted with a simple choice: either to give up their grand dreams and permit their people to go along at their own pace or to drive them with brutal force. Mercy, like tolerance, is an acquired trait, and it takes a long time for a people to develop it. Although it is nowhere as deeply and widely advanced as among the English, we find little of it among most of the present-day revolutionary leaders, who rather adhere to a philosophy resembling that of the Soviet Union. The inhuman exploitation of man which we observe in Red China, where the dictatorship of Mao Tse-tung is crushing Asians as no colonizer would ever think of doing, may well set the example for the newly freed colonial world. Up to now, twenty-one to fifty million Chinese have been murdered by their new, native, progress-minded rulers.

Today, there are approximately 647,000,000 people in the British Commonwealth, a free association of the eight sovereign and independent states of the United Kingdom: Canada, Australia, New Zealand, South Africa, India, Pakistan, and Ceylon. Together with other associated, related, or British-controlled territories, these countries occupy 14,500,000 million square miles, or about one-fourth, of the world's total land surface, and they contain about one-fourth of the world population. In many backward areas, the British Commonwealth tries to promote the establishment of the political, economic, and social high standards which would allow these areas to join the Commonwealth as sovereign members.

England has not always performed her service as colonizer for altruistic reasons, yet altruism has always played its part. Frequently, the Christian missionary has gone hand in hand with the trader, and next to the trading post, it was often a school building that was erected. Even the United States owes a great debt for its colonization by England, which gave us our system of law, as well as our sense of justice, fair play, decency, and the dignity of man. And England did not get much in return from America or, for that matter, from the other areas she occupied and developed. The purpose of the tax which brought about the Boston Tea Party and the American Revolution was not to raise funds for the King of England but to make the American colonies contribute their share to the warfare which protected them against the French and Indians from Canada. Even today the military security of the entire British Commonwealth is supported almost entirely by the taxation of the people of the British Isles, and there are other substantial sacrifices which England makes for her colonies and their natives.

Though less widely known than our Marshall Plan and its financial aid, the United Kingdom also gives such aid to its present-day colonies. Between 1920 and 1956, the total amount of economic "shots in the arm" supplied through the British Colonial Development Corporation amounted to approximately $1,347,000,000; for the period from 1955 to 1960, Parliament has allocated an additional $333,200,000 for further aid in colonial development and welfare work. Since 1945, colonial university colleges have been built by the British in East Africa, Ghana, Nigeria, the West Indies, and the Federation of Malaya, and another one is under construction in Southern Rhodesia. An older university is still doing business in Hong Kong, despite periodic Communist riots on the campus. The total number of students at these colonial university institutions runs beyond five thousand, while more than eleven thousand colonial students are studying in the British Isles.

After discussing the colonial question with leaders in the British Colonial Office, I asked them a rather cynical question. "It's very obvious," I smiled, "that you're doing your best for these colonies and you're sinking considerable money in them. But what do you expect to get out of it? Do you play, as we Americans are sometimes accused of doing, Santa Claus or Lady Bountiful?" "No!" said the British statesman. "No one would claim that we have been motivated by pure altruism in our dealings with the colonial territories. Nor would I pretend that the development toward self-government has always been seen as clearly as it is today. This new policy has only gradually taken shape, changing as men's ideas change. But the British colonization has meant peace, an end to slavery and other barbarous practices, a start of education and medical services and the growth of revenues to pay for them, the expansion of trade, better living standards to all, and, step by step, the establishment of effective governments based on democratic ideas. This is the British concept of colonialism. Today, we know that with the development of our colonies and the growth of our Commonwealth in peace and successful economic improvement, we will benefit along with them."

Whether you take the pro-colonial or the anti-colonial side, don't accept ready-made platitudes and stereotyped condemnations from those who have an ax to grind. Don't be misled by those who are pointing their damning fingers at the colonizers. In a very few years, if they're honest, they may be pounding their own chests to admit their great mistake with a *mea culpa*.

15 West Germany: Victory Over Words

When I think of Germany, the first thing to come to my mind is an adventure which a friend of mine had recently in Frankfurt. Every time he goes to a new city in a foreign land, he steps out of his hotel after checking in and boards a streetcar or a bus—any streetcar, any bus. He rides it to the end of the line and from there takes a return trip to his hotel. It is a good way to talk with strangers, see the city and its life, and get a look at foreign ways from the inside—and it's inexpensive, too.

When my friend arrived in Frankfurt, he followed his usual custom and took the first trolley that passed his hotel on the Bahnhofplatz. Unfortunately, however, the trolley would not return at the end of the line; it was to go to the carbarn for the night. When the buxom conductor noticed the lone passenger sitting in her trolley after everyone else had left, she called to him: *"Sie müssen aussteigen."* (You must get off.) My friend, who understands no German, said: "Oh, it's quite all right. I'm going to sit here and ride back with you." The conductor, who, in turn, understood no English, repeated carefully, now articulating every word: *"Steigen Sie jetzt aus; der Wagen fährt jetzt ins Depot."* (Get off now; the car is going to the carbarn.) "Well now," said my friend, "that's an interesting word, that German word *jetzt*. We have a word like that in English. It is pronounced 'yet.' Almost the same word. We have many things in common." The conductor shook her head. *"Was ist mit Ihnen los?"* (What's the matter with you?) My friend grinned good-naturedly: "Say, I'll tell you what. I'm quite willing to pay for the return ride. I usually don't, but if you insist, it's all right with me. How much do you want?" "Mister," explained the conductor in German, "you have to get off. I must push this button, nod twice to the motorman, take the car into the carbarn and leave it for the night, and hurry home to prepare dinner for my husband and my children. Get off!" "Well," said my friend, "let's keep calm about this. It's a fine day. I'm very fond of you Germans. Back in the States, we have many persons of German ancestry. As a matter of fact, I have a little German in my blood, too. Why don't you just stop this conversation now and get this trolley going back to my hotel so I can ride along and enjoy the scenery?" *"Steigen Sie endlich aus!"* snapped the conductor. "That sounds like an abrupt statement," my friend replied. "On more mature thought, you might regret this."

Now what would *you* do to end such talk? A girl running a trolley in Rome would probably take my friend by the hand, smile at him seductively as she led him down the steps, and then hop back in the trolley and close the door before he could follow her. In Paris, a situation like this would certainly lead to spirited, if not furious, exchanges, but as soon as the French conductor saw that his language wasn't understood and that his words didn't ignite action, he'd shrug his shoulders, push the button, nod twice to the motorman, and take his passenger into the carbarn along with the car. My friend could sit there all night or perhaps stumble out amidst the repair wagons, over the grease spots, and through the litter.

But this was Frankfurt, Germany. Here was a conductor who saw the futility of further conversation. If she struck my friend, that would be use of force, which isn't popular these days. If she shoved him down the steps, near which he was standing, he might fall, and that would lead to a lawsuit. If she let him sit for the night, it wouldn't be "humane." Therefore, she just gave him the hip—not a hard hip, just enough bump to send him hurrying down the steps while she closed the door, pushed the button, and nodded twice to the motorman. The conversation was ended, and the seemingly hopeless problem was solved to everybody's pleasure. My friend, a bit surprised, took the next trolley back to the hotel.

What makes this little scene so significant is the practical way in which this German woman revealed her contempt for mere words and her faith in efficient action after she had discovered that words did not bring results. In this attitude, she resembles her people, for the Germans learned the futility, if not the meaninglessness, of words during the iron rule of Hitler and in the postwar years. They have now put their trust in doing rather than talking, and what they do is efficient, practical and to the point.

The words fed to the German people during the past few decades bore, as the Germans discovered, little resemblance to reality. In addition to the lies, deceits, phony promises, and threats with which they have been—and still are—regaled by the East, they have also discovered that the words of the West tended to contradict realities. To recall a few examples (as all Germans do), they well remember how we assured them that victory over Hitler would bring the end of all wars. They remember too, how we used to preach that a soldier's life was a disgraceful series of crimes, for which reason we had all soldiers' and officers' pensions cut off in Germany. Today, though, we're begging the Germans to rearm, trying to reinoculate their soldierly spirit, and selecting a German general as a supreme commander of the North Atlantic Treaty Organization.

Nor have the Germans forgotten the Morgenthau Plan, a scheme to deprive Germany of all industrial might and reduce the nation to a slumland while we permitted the Soviet Union to cut off from West Germany the only really fertile land in what was formerly the Third Reich. They thought of us as "allies" of the Russians, but then they discovered that there was no such alliance. In fact, when I mentioned the "alliance" in 1945 to Berlin's Bishop Dibelius of the Evangelical Church, he told me that Soviet Colonel Tulpanov had just talked with him and had admonished him that the Germans must co-operate with the Communists because the Russians hated the Americans and would drive us out of Berlin.

The Germans also remember the limitations on coal and steel production which we placed upon West Germany, and so do I, after participating in countless and endless debates in the halls of the Allied Control Council. Some of the Allies became angry when the German allowance of coal to be mined was raised to ten million tons a year, but soon we ourselves were pushing German coal production, and also steel production, after we had dismantled some of the German steel plants. Today, we rely on the German economy to blaze the way for the recovery of Europe. This is the very opposite of the first orders I received when I was going into Germany at the end of the war: "Remember, Frank, this is not France. You did a great job in France for our friends. But we must crush the Germans, who are our enemies. Let them starve and stew in their own juice."

Then, too, there were the words of the American in charge of German finance, at a time when the German currency was inflated by ten times the normal amount and when, according to estimates, seventy-three billion Reichmarks instead of the normal eight billion were in circulation. He said: "Use all the new money you want. Let's fix their economy but good." In contrast to and soon after these words, we ourselves undertook the German currency reform by the exchange of ten old marks for one new mark, and we helped to establish the most solid currency of Europe.

Of course we issued bookshelves of words at the Nürnberg Trials, but while we tried and condemned German war criminals, we showed our friendship for such Russian war criminals as General Zhukov and General Sokolovsky, leaders in the rape of Berlin, one of the most hideous war crimes since the time of Genghis Khan.

How far from fact can words possibly be? The Germans who had a front seat in the great show of contemporary history wisely decided that in order to solve their problems, they should never again rely upon words, not even the multilingual, well-translated words that are mass-produced at international conferences. After they heard the optimistic wordage of such conferences at Teheran, Yalta, Potsdam, London, Moscow, Berlin, and Geneva and after they listened to our happy announcements of the progress made and the accord arrived at, they saw only that the Soviets brought home the bacon.

As a result of all these memories and experiences, the Germans decided that there was little to gain from words. Grateful though they were for foreign—particularly American—help, they knew that they had to help themselves by *doing* the necessary things themselves; that's how they have become a "do-it-yourself" nation. From this resulted their impressive economic recovery, based on solid leadership and the firm back of German labor.

One of the most illuminating reasons for what has been called Germany's economic miracle was given to me by a man who was himself actively behind much of it——my old friend Ludger Westrick, right-hand man of Economics Minister Ludwig Erhard. More than sixty-five years old by now, he constantly betrays his warm feelings of friendship for the United States, where one of his eight children lives as the wife of an American. "I'm no politician," he told me, "I'm a businessman. You asked me about the unity of Germany. It would be a wonderful thing. East Germany and West Germany complement each other economically. They, the East, have agricultural lands, and we can help them to introduce modern methods to increase production. They have electrical power we can use, since West Germany needs more power. They have brown coal, which we also need. You know, Germany imported last year more than twenty-two million tons of hard coal from the United States. You might figure this roughly as something over a quarter of a million dollars' worth."

While Westrick went on, in his enthusiastic manner, to tell me of the growth of West German industries, I thought of the changes this growth has brought about. Westrick explained to me his country's present shortage of manpower, but only a little while ago, in 1950 to be exact, the then German Minister for Marshall Plan Affairs, Franz Blücher, told me of the tremendous difficulties he faced merely to keep alive the ten million refugees living in West Germany. While most of them are now gainfully employed, there aren't enough people around to work for industrially revived West Germany.

I asked Westrick what had accounted for Germany's recovery. His answer was practical and simple. "First," he said, "the United States helped us when we were not in a position to help ourselves, and we will never forget it. Second, we were in such desperate shape that, by force of necessity, all Germans had to work hard and co-operate fully. Third, much of our old equipment had been destroyed by the war or hauled away as reparations. This seemed bad at the time, but as it turned out, it was a good thing." To illustrate this point, he told of his recent visit to a metallurgical plant in Czechoslovakia where the old machinery, which had been taken from West Germany after the war, became worthless because it could not compete with the new metallurgical equipment now used in West Germany. As the fourth reason for the recovery, Westrick pointed to the system of private enterprise. "When the Suez situation came along," he recalled, "there was great pressure on us from the Socialists to ration oil and gas. They love rationing and state control. I hate it. It's psychologically bad, too."

The Germans found a way to keep their oil and gas supplies, as well as their free-enterprise system. Immediately after Colonel Nasser's seizure of the Suez Canal, they arranged with the Esso Company to import large quantities of Venezuelan oil, although it cost much more than near eastern oil. As its price went up, so did the price of the local German oils, which supply 30 per cent of all German consumption. When the Suez Canal was completely blocked, the Germans had in storage more than a three months' supply and were able to announce that there would be no rationing. At the time, a motorist drove up to a gas station and nervously asked if he could buy fifty liters of gas. "Why, of course," said the attendant, "or would you rather have two hundred liters? But if you want more than that, you'll have to bring along your own container to move it." "Well," said the motorist, "I guess I'll take just ten liters. That's all I need, and I see there's plenty here."

This economic stabilization was possible only against a background of political stability, and its achievement must be largely credited to one party, Chancellor Konrad Adenauer's Christian Democratic Union (CDU), West Germany's most powerful political body. When I met with *Herren* Krone, Gerstenmaier, and Albers, three CDU leaders in the Bundestag, I inquired about the chances of political reunification of East and West Germany;

I quoted Khrushchev's statement that the question of East-West German unification was a German problem. "How can it be a German problem," Gerstenmaier objected, "since the East German government is simply a tool of the Soviet Union?" I asked him whether he thought the Soviets would agree to a united Germany if both East and West Germany had a single currency and if each carried out its own elections, while both would agree to military neutrality. "How can there be a common currency," answered Gerstenmaier excitedly as Krone nodded in agreement, "while East Germany is as completely controlled by the Soviets as it is now? How could there be fair elections in East Germany while it is held down by Soviet troops and German Communist policemen? The problem can only be solved by Germans when the Germans in East Germany are allowed, without Russian interference, freely to express all their wishes."

One of the main objections to this procedure is the Communist claim—often echoed by Western critics—that there has taken place in West Germany a "revival of German militarism." I searched for an answer among the military leaders of present-day Germany. One of them, a young man serving on what is the nearest thing to a German general staff—and an army without a general staff is not worth a toot—was a trained lawyer. "Our new German army is truly new in many regards," he explained. "The relationships between the officers and men which now prevail would have been undreamed of in the old army." One story has it that a group of enlisted men woke their commanding officer and got him out of bed to have him settle a discussion on the rights and wrongs of compulsory military service. The German officer readily gave them his views. But if the new German army could be even more fully integrated into the international NATO army, with small units of all nations—French, British, American, German, and so forth—working together, it would have far-reaching social and cultural benefits, some German officers feel.

The German army consists of approximately 120,000 men right now, and it expects to have more than 300,000 by 1960. Many problems arise as this new army, with a new spirit, is built from the ground up. However, German youth has accepted the idea of military service; the slogan *Ohne mich,* that is, "count me out," which had been so popular a short while ago, is hardly ever heard now. I thought of this growing spirit of military co-operation, or teamwork, on the road between Frankfurt and Bonn, where three strapping young Germans were thumbing for a ride. In the United States, such boys would take turns thumbing or would thumb in a disorganized manner, but these three really got attention as they moved their thumbs from left to right in perfect unison. It should not be difficult to forge youngsters like these into good soldiers.

Germany is undoubtedly on its way to strength again, although it hesitates to translate this strength into power. And there is no doubt that we cannot forego using this strength as the cornerstone of our European defense. From the military, economic, and political points of view, it is a godsend to our external security that we can rely today on the new Germany as a partner and friend.

To keep Germany's partnership, we must make a continuous effort not to alienate the new nation. What seems most imperative is for us to prove to the Germans—once again, by our actions rather than by our words—that we feel as closely tied to them as we want them to feel tied to us. In practical terms, this means that we must not cut down on our defense forces stationed on German soil or seem ready to compromise and sacrifice German interests to Soviet demands. Only if Germany feels deserted by this country or if it sees evidence for the fear that this country will end its resistance to Communism and, instead, appease the Soviets is there a danger that Germany will do exactly these things on its side, that is, desert the West. If we want the Germans to trust us, we must trust them.

PART FOUR
Front Lines of the Fight for Freedom

16

West Berlin: Western Success Story

If West Germany is the scene of an economic miracle then we are witnessing an all-around miracle in present-day Berlin. That Berlin has survived as a free city would be miraculous enough, but that today it is again a truly great city must seem almost incredible to anyone who has known it over the past fourteen years. Founded in the thirteenth century, Berlin never seemed to give much promise of the decisive industrial, commercial, and governmental roles it would play in the later history of Europe. It wasn't located on any major river, nor was it located near important deposits of coal or iron. Its geographic location was favorable, but everything else about it was literally created from nothing.

When Hitler's Third Reich surrendered on May 7, 1945, Allied bombardments and Soviet cannonades had reduced Berlin to a pile of rubble. On February 3, 1945, in less than one hour, more than a thousand acres of the thickly populated boroughs of Berlin-Mitte and Kreuzberg had been turned into a single sea of flames. A total of 35 per cent of Berlin's one and one-half million dwellings were destroyed; over 50 per cent of its many bridges were down; 20 per cent of its schools and 75 per cent of its theaters, concert halls, and other public buildings were in ruins; and 90 per cent of Berlin's prewar industrial capacity no longer existed.

This, then, was the condition of the once great city of Berlin when I entered it on June 17, 1945. I found the streets cluttered beyond passage, the people starving, and many dying from an epidemic of dysentery. During the month of July, 92 per cent of all the babies born in Berlin died within the first ten days of their lives. It seemed as if the wrath of God had been turned loose on the city, with Soviet troops following close behind, raping, stealing, killing. Hundreds of thousands—literally beyond count—lay buried in charred homes and apartments, and the sickly sweet smell of decaying bodies was everywhere.

To compare the Berlin of those frightful days with the Berlin of today leads us to the miracle I mentioned earlier. Today's Berliners are healthy, fairly well housed, and engaged in a vast program to make their city the capital of a future free and resurrected Germany. When I flew into Berlin last year, my recollections of those days, of the Soviet-imposed hunger blockade and the airlift which defeated it, did not seem to fit into the new, proud reality of the city which I now encountered. As U.S. commandant, I had been directly responsible for our share in the Berlin fight under the over-all orders of General Lucius Clay, who at that time was U.S. commanding general and high commissioner for the American Zone of Germany. On the Allied side, my corresponding members during the blockade were unflinching British General Bourne and brilliant French General Ganeval, while the U.S.S.R. was represented by General Kotakov, who, in turn, acted on orders of his superior, Generals Sokolovsky and Zhukov. It was during the blockade that the city of Berlin had its greatest moment in history and in it brought to life a new German concept of democracy. The Berliners, first and foremost of whom was the late Ernst Reuter, helped us to make this victory come to pass. Yet even they hardly dared to hope, in their most optimistic moods, for what has been achieved today; their city is not only free but is becoming beautiful, at least in the Allied sectors.

For a first-hand explanation of the vast building program of present-day West Berlin, I called on Senatsdirektor Schneevoigt, who is in charge of construction and housing. I was rather surprised when I walked into his impressive office and heard him say: "Remember me, General? We used to go birdshooting in the fields below Tempelhof." Sure enough, it was my old friend with the baggy pants, formerly a modest borough director of construction. All he and we could do in the days just after the war was to make Berlin's existing dwellings habitable with hasty patches. Today, Schneevoigt is one of the world's outstanding city planners. In a room next to his office, he pointed out Berlin's future construction plans. Here, in miniature, stood a model of the Berlin of today and tomorrow, with old buildings painted gray and newly constructed ones yellow, while proposed structures were painted white.

Today, Berlin's streets are wider, the subways run efficiently, and many new hospitals and schools keep pace with the public need. With imagination, talent, and determination, you can rebuild an almost destroyed city into an all but new city, as the Germans are proving in Berlin. The world's best city planners have contributed their ideas, and the most famed international architects have been commissioned to construct new buildings. Le Corbusier of Paris designed a seventeen-story building, now completed; Alvar Aalto of Helsinki produced a fascinating eight-story house; Walter Gropius of Cambridge, Massachusetts, designed an interesting, long ground plan structure with sixty-seven apartments and a one-story annex for commercial use. Hans Müller of Berlin, Oscar Niemeyer of Rio do Janiro, Hugh Stubbins of the United States, Arne Jacobsen of Copenhagen, Alexander Klein of Israel—in short, all the best names of modern architecture, fifty-seven of them altogether—are busy building a new Berlin.

I inspected one of these outstanding buildings in company with the brilliant young American designer, Hugh Stubbins. Called Congress Hall, it is to serve as a combined commercial and cultural center for international conferences and important commercial conventions. Bernard Gimbel, president of the New York Convention and Visitors Bureau, would be happy to have a building of its splendor in, say, Central Park. It cost approximately four and a quarter million dollars, half supplied by the United States, the other half by the Federal Republic of Germany and the city of Berlin. Eleanor Dulles, special adviser to the chief of the German Department of the U.S. Foreign Service and sister of John Foster Dulles, had a lion's share in bringing about this project. Sensibly utilitarian inside, Congress Hall is simply sensational on the outside. The Berliners, with their ever-ready sharp wit, nicknamed it because of its unusual form "The Pregnant Oyster" or, better yet, "The Ski Jump."

Berliners, not unlike New Yorkers, are endowed with a strong sense of humor, which they like to apply to the oddities of their city. One church, with an exposed framework spire resembling a skeleton, is known as "Saint Skeleton's Church." A second, modernistic church, slightly reminiscent of the pre-blockade Nissen huts which were constructed in Berlin's British sector, is called "Saint Nissen." The three bells of another church, which were donated by the cities of Bremen, Hamburg, and Lübeck, have been dubbed "Faith, Hope, and Charity."

Fast approaching self-sufficiency with its 110 per cent increase in industry since the blockade, Berlin would already be completely self-sufficient were it not for the systematic Communist counter-measures against it. In contrast, the United States has played a very important and active part in Berlin's revival. One of the many American contributions is the Berlin Memorial Library, a newly constructed, ideally designed German library given to the city of Berlin by the United States when John J. McCloy was high commissioner as a permanent and practical memorial to the Berliners' courage in resisting the Soviet-imposed hunger blockade. Including the books in its stacks, it cost approximately $1,200,000. When U.S. Ambassador James B. Conant dedicated it, he stated: "The response of the Berlin public to this type of library service has justified the decisions of those Germans and Americans responsible for the use of the special American fund set aside for a memorial to German-American co-operation during the Berlin blockade days when democracy was being tested." Although this magnificent library, where self-service is a new thing for German libraries, displays no American propaganda, it does teach the fundamentals of democracy as we know and cherish them by making available a world of knowledge. It contrasts, as is our intent, with the Soviet House of Culture, a sorry state propaganda mill in Berlin's Soviet sector.

The Amerika Haus in Berlin is a modern structure that is

similar to the Berlin Memorial Library in appearance. Offering information and facts about America's science, culture, industry, and way of life and run by the U.S. Information Agency, the Amerika Haus seems to function in accordance with President Eisenhower's proclamation that "it is not enough for us to have sound policies dedicated to goals of universal peace, freedom and progress. These policies must be made known to and understood by all people throughout the world. This is the responsibility of the U.S. Information Agency." Of its total cost of approximately $250,000, the United States granted approximately $200,000, while the city of Berlin agreed to supply the site, services, architectural design, utilities, landscaping, and other features.

The Amerika Haus was a surprise to me after seeing our information center on the market place at Accra, Ghana. It has grown to its present size from the small center I helped to dedicate in a poor section of Berlin near the Russian sector in February, 1946. Although it is still too early to judge its results, its projection room, its reference library, and its facilities for youth groups, if properly directed, can do a great job for future German-American relations. If improperly directed, it will be a waste of American money and Germany energy. I can only hope that the State Department will bear in mind that such important information centers, scattered about the world, are not proper receptacles for disgruntled career officers who are unacquainted with the subtleties of education and propaganda. When for a time combat officers who hadn't made good were dumped into military government, we paid the price for this fallacy; it would be well for the State Department to benefit from our experiences.

The most spectacular product of German-American co-operation in Berlin is the Free University. Today, it is a going concern where approximately ten thousand students are pursuing courses in almost all of the humanities and the sciences. Arrangements are being made to obtain a simple, college-type atomic reactor for scientific study, probably similar in kind to that used at the New York University College of Engineering.

The Free University has gone far since its inception in 1947. At the time of the blockade, the students of East Berlin's Soviet-dominated University of Berlin felt the need for a new university. More than one thousand students held a mass meeting in the Soviet sector to protest the low quality and political character of their education. The meeting was broken up by Communist police, and eight of the leading boys and girls were arrested, never again to be seen. A delegation came to me (I was U.S. commandant in Berlin at the time) to suggest that a new university be established in the Western sector. Their request, which I forwarded and recommended to higher headquarters, dragged on for many months, opposed by the American educational advisers for Germany. A new university could not be established, these so-called experts claimed, because qualified professors would stay away from it, only inferior students would attend such a school without a long-established reputation, and besides, where would the books come from, how could we have a university without buildings, and so on to a hundred other objections.

Perhaps some of these arguments came from Communist sources. But thanks to U.S. Commander General Lucius Clay, a sum of three million dollars was finally appropriated to set up the new school. Today, approximately one-third of all its students come from the East German sector of Berlin and the Eastern zone of Germany. Particularly for them, a new student village is under construction. It will house several hundred refugee students and will contribute to the human understanding and tolerance which grows from the close social relationships of college days. The most outstanding of the present buildings is the Henry Ford Library, made possible some years ago by a gift of one million dollars from the Ford Foundation. Its dedication in 1954 occasioned my return to Berlin, where the Free University awarded me a doctorate of medicine *honoris causa*. As the then Dean of the Medical School Professor Fischer proclaimed, this was to honor the service performed by the Americans under my command during the early days of the occupation, when we successfully fought disease and epidemic throughout Berlin.

Not all of the Berlin refugees are students. Since 1952, more than 1,300,000 refugees from Communism have escaped to the West through Berlin. According to estimates, a total of more than

3,000,000 have escaped from the East to West Germany across the border. These refugees are now welcomed with open arms by the West, since there is a high percentage of skilled workers and young persons among them. In 1953, the highest point of the refugee movement, 305,737 escaped to the Western side of Berlin. Right now, about 2,000 a week are passing through Berlin.

I visited one of the refugee camps in 1957, or, more precisely, I visited an old family friend named Louise. From 1945 to 1949, when my wife, Edith, our four children, and I lived in Berlin, Louise had been our cook. Upon arriving in Berlin in 1957, I received a small bouquet of flowers and a note from her saying that she now lived and worked in the refugee camp as a cook director. Living in a refugee camp is not much of a life. I've had quite a bit of experience with refugee camps, camps of Arabs, Jews, anti-Communist fighters, and I've even inspected them on the island of Formosa after the Free Chinese had abandoned the Tachen Islands. They're miserable places at best, places of crying children, bewildered women, and determined men. There must be a better way to provide for the victims of tyranny than putting them in refugee camps.

To some degree, refugee camps are the product of our past failures. When we first went to Berlin, the Americans, French, and British, jointly with Russians, controlled the city. At first the German government of the city was appointed by the Soviets, who had been allowed to capture Berlin while we sat at the Elbe and waited. Only after we insisted were city-wide elections held on the twentieth of October, 1946. Their outcome left no doubt that the people of Berlin rejected Communism. From that moment on, the Communists tried by means of pressure, intimidation, threat, and harassment to regain control of the elected city government, but the Berlin officials and their people stood firm, while the British, French, and Americans supported the elected representatives. The Soviet Union, although it was bound by treaty to recognize this government, reacted instead with its blockade of Berlin. It was an attempt to gain complete control of the city of Berlin by starving the people into submission and by driving out the Western powers. But the Soviets failed in their attempt to win by force and settled for their control of one-third of the city, which they still hold.

This is the usual story of Soviet aggression. It was practiced when the Communists attempted to take all of Korea and then, after we had defeated their purpose, settled for keeping half of Korea; they repeated the same strategy in Indochina and in Germany. When and where we have succeeded in defeating them, we tend to throw away the victory at the conference table. Although our position may not seem very courageous, it has turned out to be rather practical, for both the Germans and the Allies want the physical presence of Western troops in the city of Berlin, not that the city could be held against the Soviet army, but our troops back up the word of our diplomats and keep the growing democracy of West Berlin from being crushed by Communist aggression. The Berlin garrison stands to prove our will to defend Berlin, whatever the moment's administrations and policies in Washington might be, and demonstrates clearly that any attack upon this city means war with the United States, Great Britain, and France. The Soviets are well aware of the fact that our brilliantly commanded elite troops in Berlin would fight—win, lose, or draw—and therefore they won't attack unless or until they find it to their advantage to precipitate World War III, which they will probably not do in the foreseeable future.

To Berliners, the American GI is now a part of the population, and they accept him as a neighbor. He and his civilian dependants pretty much live their own lives in an American way, mind their own business, and generally enjoy good relationships with the Germans wherever they have occasion for contact. Their departure from Berlin would be a psychological catastrophe in German eyes and an invitation for new Soviet aggression.

Berlin is not out of the economic and political woods. It must still be supported by West Germany to the tune of approximately one billion marks a year (about $250,000,000). There are many stumbling blocks along the road of progress, and although "there's many a slip 'twixt the cup and the lip," I trust that Berlin will again be one of the greatest cities in Europe, with or without consent from foreign powers.

At any rate, the miracle of Berlin has impressively proved two things which may be incorporated into our foreign-policy pattern in general. First, the Soviets must retreat if and when we resist their designs with our whole military, economic, political, and psychological might, as we did when we responded with the airlift to their challenge of the blockade. Second, we can resist the Soviets when we support our foreign friends, who hate Communism as much as we do in this country. Since we have proved to the Berliners that we stand by them, they will stand by us. From this common resistance against the enemy and from this common effort to strengthen the values of the West comes Berlin's miracle of success.

"Can the Soviets drive us out of Berlin?" It's an old, old record: they never quit trying. Since 1945, when we arrived in Berlin as part of an international agreement, the Soviets have been trying to drive us out. We gave them rich land—Saxony, Thuringia, and a chunk of land running all the way to Czechoslovakia—as the price for our going to Berlin. They kept what we gave them, and they have been trying to take our share of Berlin ever since.

Before and during the elections of October 20, 1946, the Soviets revived their efforts to drive us out. There were threats, kidnappings, whispered warnings over cocktails that they were determined to get us out; they raided the U.S. sector to show us who was boss. They even cut off the electricity so that the people of Berlin would realize who was really in control of the city and what would happen if they voted against the Communist party, which they promptly did at the rate of eight to two. Hermann Mattern, that evil, ignorant, fanatic, Number 2 man of the Communist party in East Berlin, had the audacity during the blockade of Berlin to indicate that the Americans, British, and French and their families would be put in concentration camps for later disposal, as soon, presumably, as the Soviets occupied all of Berlin.

Mattern I remember well. Some time after his insult, we succeeded in catching him in the U.S. sector, where he owned a house. He was brought before me to explain his part in the production of a scurrilous booklet attacking the Americans. It was called "Gangsters at Work." Mildly, and with an air of innocence,

I asked Mattern for his explanation of this extraordinary booklet. He gave me a great line but admitted his responsibility, along with the responsibility of the Soviet Cultural Affairs officer who had approved the broadside. When I got through telling Mattern what I might do to him unless he had a satisfactory apology and explanation within forty-eight hours, the smug expression was gone from his face. The apology and explanation, such as it was, was in on time. Now, in 1959, Mattern is again singing the theme of the Communists: that we have no right in Berlin, that we had better get out, that, specifically, the commercial airlines flying into Berlin have no right to do so. He is ready to back up his threats, for it is known that experimentation is taking place along the normal air routes in preparation of jamming our radio beams, without which commercial and military planes cannot fly into Berlin during the fog-shrouded winter months.

Now, in 1959, after Khrushchev's ultimatum to the Western powers to get out of Berlin, we face some very serious problems. He indicates the Soviet army's intention of withdrawing from all of Germany and turning over all controls, including the "say" over Berlin, to the Communist-imposed government of East Berlin and East Germany. "Make West Berlin, if you will," says he, "a free city." "This is another Soviet trick to destroy our freedom," says West Berlin's courageous mayor, Willy Brandt. "Never, never!" swear the crisis-hardened people of West Berlin.

Khrushchev's proposal, aside from its complete dishonesty and its absolute illegality, is colossal crust. By agreement, all of Berlin is supposed to be under four-power control. At the end of the blockade, because we did not insist upon our rights, the Soviets succeeded in detaching from Allied control one-third of the city. But Khrushchev isn't talking about living up to his old agreements and restoring his third to Allied control. He's now giving us suggestions about what to do with the remaining two-thirds, West Berlin, still under the control of the Allies.

What we think of Khrushchev's proposal has been clearly stated by President Eisenhower: "We stand firm on the rights and the responsibilities that we have undertaken." It has also been stated by Secretary of State Dulles: "The Soviet rulers, in relation to Berlin, seek to repudiate a whole series of agreements. They seem to feel at liberty to denounce, at their pleasure, any agreements which they have made, as soon as they feel that these agreements no longer serve their purposes." Former President Harry S. Truman, no beginner in dealings with the Soviets, puts his feelings on the matter in this manner: "Whether Khrushchev's ultimatum to force the West to accept repudiation of the Four Power Agreement, by the trick proposal of a Free City of West Berlin, is a maneuver to force recognition of East Germany, or another in the series of provocative acts to harass us, we cannot permit them to get away with it."

How does a government, the chief executive of which is Dwight D. Eisenhower, arrive at a decision that we will not get out of Berlin under Soviet ultimatum? The process is very simple. It follows a military pattern of thinking: a thorough and continuous estimate of the situation is made. Such an estimate has undoubtedly been made since my departure from Berlin in 1949. The estimators of the situation bear in mind our mission in Berlin. They consider all the opposing forces of the Soviets versus the Westerners: military strength, economic strength, all strengths and weaknesses. They take into consideration everything which the Soviets and their Communist stooges might do to drive us from Berlin or cause us to leave. They match against those things everything that we can do to maintain our position there, to uphold our prestige, in short, to accomplish our mission. Finally, the process boils down to a decision. After the decision is made, complete and detailed plans are worked out to meet every situation and to produce certain situations of our own liking.

The moderate, middle-of-the-road policy of our government would suggest that the Soviets be told calmly that we will not get out of Berlin. This has been done. It would provide for a great number of counter-punches. This is not necessarily defensive thinking; it is simply striking back in answer to specific actions which may be taken against us by the Soviets or by the Communist-controlled government of East Germany, through which our lines of communication run to Berlin. We could list here a great number of possible actions on the part of the Soviets or the East

German government and possible answers to them. If the road is blocked, will we send through armored convoys? If this, if that—these "ifs" appear and will continue to appear in American newspapers until the problem is solved.

There are, however, much broader fields of speculation and planning. What, for example, will we do if the Soviets do withdraw their 400,000 troops from East Germany and rioting results? Will we of the West send troops to restore order and, incidentally, support the democratic forces? Or will we stand idly by while the Soviet troops march in and destroy our friends, as they did in Hungary?

Suppose, in Berlin, where we have never been relieved of our postwar responsibilities for all of Berlin, as well as for West Berlin, the Soviets carry out their expressed intention of reneging on their obligations and rioting results. Will we stand by while either Soviet troops or the East German Communist army march in and shoot up the place? Or will we, with perfect legality, send British, French, and American troops into East Berlin to restore order and, incidentally, protect our friends, who will have made short work of the Communist stooge government?

What if the East German army, the People's Police, stages a military junta, killing their Communist overlords and appealing to West Germany for immediate union? What will our action be? What can we expect the action of the West German army to be if the Soviet army comes back into East Germany and launches a reign of terror?

Make no mistake about it, the people of East Germany, as well as East Berlin, hate their Communist overlords and their Soviet rulers. I, for one, would expect that within months after the withdrawal of Soviet troops from East Germany, the German people would again rise up, even at the risk of their lives, to regain their freedom.

17 East Berlin to Budapest: The Need for More Than Words

Since Khrushchev set out to use for reaching his old and never changing Communist goal of world conquest, new and streamlined methods of salesmanship and persuasion, Americans have had a chance to travel to the Soviet realm. One American magazine appealed to U.S. tourists to visit Soviet Russia, whose scenic and artistic attractions it described in a rather lurid article, with no mention of Russia's less attractive sights, such as concentration camps, secret police, and permanent terror. In similar fashion, the travel bureaus of the Soviet satellite nations advertise in our free press in order to lure the readers of America's Sunday papers to their lands. And foreign correspondents are going to all the capitals of Communism, from Moscow to East Berlin, for a censored look at what the Communists want them to see. The Soviet empire is again on the travel map.

Whether tourists—and even most foreign correspondents—get to see more and other things than the Soviet leaders want them to see is doubtful. What is certain is that the peoples of the Soviet-oppressed countries have themselves gone all out, sometimes at the risk of their lives, to let the West see very clearly what they feel and what they aspire to without the need of a single tourist or correspondent visiting them at home.

What these peoples have communicated to the West has one single meaning: "We want to be free!" In clear and unmistakable language, often underlined with their own blood, and whenever the slightest opportunity seemed to beckon, they have admonished the West not to fall for the verbiage of their own Communist propaganda media, often echoed by well-meaning and not-so-well-meaning Western "experts." The peoples of the Soviet East ask the West to disbelieve that they have become Communists, want things to stay as they are in their countries, and despise the values of the West. "We want the same rights to life, liberty, and pursuit of happiness which you have in the West." This is the message that the people of Soviet-dominated lands have signaled across the Iron Curtain over and over again in the past few years.

Nobody could mistake these signals when they came, first from East Berlin and then from all of East Germany, where the people began to rebel against their Soviet masters in June, 1953. At that time, the workers rose up against their masters, and then the rest of the population joined them. I talked with many East Germans, both before this uprising and after it. Some had joined Communist organizations under pressure or for the sake of convenience, but few joined because of personal conviction that it was "right." When Soviet reality showed itself in its true colors, to contradict and ridicule in every detail the very promises of Communist words, the people rebelled. Only Soviet tanks—not words—won a victory for Communism.

From 1953 on, hardly a year has gone by without another uprising of Communist-dominated people against Communist rulers. While the struggle in East Germany raged, news of uprisings came from Poznań and other Polish cities, from Pilsen and other Czech towns, and from Soviet Russia itself, where, in universities and in forced-labor camps, the protest of free people was audibly voiced, even when, particularly when, the Communists tried to placate them by granting minor concessions. As soon as economic and political conditions were eased slightly, these peoples felt that perhaps the moment had come when their rulers had weakened; they demanded more, much more than the rulers could grant without undermining their own strength, and clashes, protests, revolt, and suppression followed.

This was the way in which the Hungarian uprising of October, 1956, began. Its story need not be retold; in a few brief, glorious weeks, a whole people rose against the Soviets to demand na-

tional, spiritual, and political freedom. Once again, only Soviet
tanks and Soviet terror could win the victory for the Communists.
Communist bullets killed Hungarian men, women and children—
this is how Communism keeps its power.

But if the struggle of the satellite peoples, in one form or another, is almost certain to continue, so will its impact on our own
foreign policy remain strong. What we should do, or whether we
should do anything at all, about their struggle remains probably
the most difficult and perhaps the most decisive question of our
policy with regard to foreign countries. It poses questions which
the people under Soviet rule, from East Berlin to Budapest to
Moscow, have asked us, which we must answer, and which we
hardly have answered yet, except by evasion, postponement, and
unfortunate wordage.

First, do we have a right to get mixed up in the struggle for
liberation of the oppressed? The question is different from that
of the colonial peoples, which could be answered with the conclusion that we must let them work out their own destinies, since
we have little right, reason, or interest to assist them against their
colonial rulers. The question is different in the case of the Soviet-
ruled nations because we are bound by moral and legal ties to
defend their rights. In the wartime and postwar agreements of
the Allies, we have firmly and solemnly promised them the freedom to choose their own destiny. But after this promise, we have
given in to the Communist co-signer and ex-ally who has deprived
them of these rights by force and violence and imposed on them
a destiny which they never chose.

The second question would be whether we have a duty to do
something on behalf of these peoples. The answer is again affirm-
ative, and it has been reaffirmed in words by the American government ever since the problem came up. If this is a legal point,
it concerns our word given as a commitment, and if we disregard
it, we cannot expect other peoples to trust us any more than they
trust the Soviets. Yet what we have done so far, or so it seems to
me, was mainly, if not only, to back up our word by words rather
than to act in accordance with our word. As early as 1952, we
announced our policy of liberation, which, although it was care-

fully worded, was bound to be understood as a promise to act on behalf of captive peoples, and this was not altogether a misunderstanding. This policy, which had been a plank in the party platforms of 1952, became a part of governmental policy, and it was, to some degree at least, from confidence in this policy that the captive peoples rebelled to throw off the yokes of their Soviet masters.

After 1953, I was to hear again and again from many East German freedom fighters that it had been the propaganda of RIAS, the American-directed radio station in West Berlin that beams daily programs to the East Germans, which had given them courage to rise. But when they did rise, we simply stood by and even went out of our way to demonstrate our neutrality. In fact, we gave the East Germans—as well as the other peoples behind the Iron Curtain who were watching us and waiting for our action—the impression that we not only failed to back up our words with corresponding deeds but that we systematically backed out of our positions.

The same thing, but in larger measure, happened when the Hungarians revolted against Soviet power. While victory seemed close to the rebels, they, and with them the free world, thought we would come to their aid; this was what they expected after listening to Voice of America broadcasts. But we did not do much as they were defeated; our action boiled down to speeches and relief for those who could escape and more words in the United Nations Assembly and elsewhere. To many Americans, to most people behind the Iron Curtain, to a large number of free men everywhere, this seemed a record of sadness, if not shame.

Since our propaganda media had told listeners behind the Iron Curtain not to make their peace with or surrender to Communism, they had concluded that we advised them to resist. From this it was only a very small step to the next conclusion: that we were not only favoring their resistance but would also actively support it. They assumed that we meant what we said and would act accordingly.

True, we did not incite these people, in so many words, to rebel, as has been claimed after Berlin and again after Hungary.

Our propaganda media, particularly the American-supported radio stations beaming their messages behind the Iron Curtain, were very careful to avoid this special message. Painstaking investigations have led to a full refutation of the charge that the Voice of America had promised American support to the Hungarian freedom fighters, as some of them and Communist propaganda machinery claimed. What happened was that some Hungarians, in the excitement of battle, thought they had heard such a pronouncement. People often hear what they want to hear, and it was understandable that some Hungarians heard more from their radios than we actually said. But it was even less true that, as the Communist propaganda machinery also claimed, America, through its "agents," "undercover apparatus," and "spy organizations," had a hand in and even instigated, directed, and led the uprisings. From thoroughgoing interrogations of all the leading participants and from serious historical accounts undertaken by neutral researchers and by such neutral organizations as the United Nations *Ad Hoc* Committee, it has been established beyond a doubt that the uprising in Hungary, as in East Germany and elsewhere, was spontaneous. Its members were local citizens who had no contacts with foreign countries or agents, American or otherwise.

These movements of rebellion were sadly lacking in leadership. In Hungary, the rebels ranged from confused, wavering, naïvely half-disillusioned and half-hopeful Communists like Imre Nagy, who felt, up to the last minute, that the Soviets would give in to their demands, to the young, inexperienced, politically helpless students of the Petofi Circle, who started the rebellion when they demanded more freedom for their discussions and scientific training. Old, traditional trends of freedom and faith, which the Communists could not uproot, helped the uprising to flare up. Hungary, after all, has a long and proud record of fights in defense of freedom and faith.

When the Soviet army drove the Nazis out of Hungary, it was welcomed as a liberator. But the Hungarians soon learned that a tiger had been driven out and a bear welcomed in. The Soviet rape, pillage, and looting of Hungary filled the Hungarians with antagonism and opposition. The Russians didn't know that, however. Having promised (at Yalta) free elections in order to obtain Allied acquiescence to their occupation of Hungary, the Soviets did permit such in 1945, but instead of a rousing victory for Communism, their hand-picked stooges won only 17 per cent of the votes cast.

I was in Berlin as U.S. commandant at the time, and I watched the repercussions of the Communist defeat in Hungary as they were felt in our Berlin Allied Kommandatura. After the Americans arrived in Berlin during the summer of 1945, we planned to let the Germans hold free elections as soon as we had weeded out the remaining Nazis. But the Hungarian election of November 4, 1945, put a damper on Soviet enthusiasm for elections. Month after month of negotiations went by, and dodge after dodge was employed by the Soviet commanders to avoid an election in Berlin, to which they had agreed and which was, in fact, one of the reasons for our occupation. While Soviet commandants came and went, their answers to our inquiries for elections was ever the same *"Nyet."* Finally, in the late spring of 1946, the British, French, and Americans insisted that the Soviet commandant, General Kotakov, set a date, no matter how far off, on which the city might have its elections. He replied that it would be meaningless to set a date, that if he said, for instance, next Christmas, it wouldn't mean anything. No election would be held in Berlin until the Soviets were certain that reactionary forces would not win, as they had in Hungary. Further questioning brought out the fact that practically every voter who opposed Communism was considered by the Soviets to be a reactionary.

If the Hungarians have a national tradition filled with proud memories of their fight for freedom, other peoples behind the Iron Curtain have similar traditions, along with a thirst for freedom. It is this perennial opposition to tyranny which can never win a people with its actions, whether it has first seduced them with its words or not, that underlies revolt behind the Iron Curtain and makes it reasonably certain that such struggle will flare up again as long as people are people, that is, as long as there are men in search of human rights and natural rights, a fact which Communists have not succeeded in abolishing anywhere.

Surely it is to our interest, in addition to our honor and duty, to help the Soviet slaves. In the first place, a decisive weakening of the enemy is at least as much a victory for us as would be a primary move to strengthen our own side. If the peoples behind the Iron Curtain rebel against their masters, it means both a decisive weakening of Soviet power and a decisive strengthening of our side. On the military plane, the Soviet armies are considerably reduced in strength if the satellite troops cannot be trusted by the Moscow masters, and what is more, they must use their trustworthy troops to hold down and, if need be, fight the enemies in their own lands. On a political and psychological plane, the permanent rebellion of the people against their Soviet-controlled governments, which oppress them in incomparably worse ways than would "capitalists" or "colonialists," is bound to prove to many innocents abroad the true nature of Communism. The defections which the Communists have suffered, after Hungary, in France, Italy, England, and, to some degree, Asia have proved this point. If one or more of these rebellions could lead to a victory of the freedom fighters, it would have more positive results for the free world than many other events for which we strive and sacrifice. But it is probable that in order to achieve this, these peoples need more help from the West than they have received up to now.

There remains, therefore, a third—the most difficult—question: What can we do to help them and at the same time promote our own best interests? The question can be put in a slightly more concrete form: Which actions are we willing and prepared to undertake in order to back up our words and therefore what words should we choose when we address ourselves to the peoples behind the Iron Curtain?

During the past few years, our governmental media have made it a practice to tell peoples behind the Iron Curtain only facts, that is, facts about the cruel and terroristic nature of their rulers and facts about the economic, political, and spiritual "better life" in the West, particularly in the United States. This can certainly not do any harm, but the question is whether it does much good. People behind the Iron Curtain know, at least as well as broadcasters and researchers on our side, all about their system, and they do not have to be told how horrible it is. They see these facts first hand in every waking hour of their lives. In turn, we are not certain that the tales of the good Western life mean much to them; most of them are already convinced that life in freedom is much better than theirs, and to be told so by those who enjoy it, without hope for them to partake of it, too, often tends to antagonize them. How would you feel if you were a half-starved pauper and a rich uncle constantly told you about his fortune and the happiness it gave him? How would you feel if you were perennially in fear of terrorists and somebody told you how quiet and secure his community was? If he would not assist you in making your own way toward this better life, chances are you would soon come to resent him.

Groups independent from our government—for instance, Russian refugees, organized in their NTS (Union of National Solidarity), or the broadcasters of Radio Liberation in Munich, or East German refugee groups, or the Assembly of Captive Nations, which comprises other refugee groups—go farther on their own. They send to captive peoples messages or contact them through underground liaisons in order to tell them that change must be brought about. But here is another question. In the end, a decisive change can be brought about only by force against the Soviet rulers, who never have abdicated anywhere of their own free will. As previous events have shown, they can be overthrown only by their own weakness or by the superior strength of their adversaries. But liberation is close if and when the Soviet troops themselves appear so unreliable and impregnated by revolutionary ideas that they would fraternize with rather than shoot rebels. Do avenues of action open here for us? Is it possible for us—by means of propaganda, contacts, the underground, or other liaison—to work on these troops, who are today Moscow's last and only means of rule and who may tomorrow be gravediggers for the Communist leaders?

Furthermore, liberation is close if and when the West joins its force with the force of the rebels. This we did not do in East Germany, Hungary, or elsewhere. We were afraid it might lead to a shooting war, which we want to avoid. Whether this risk was great has been much debated, and it seems doubtful that it would have precipitated an all-out war. Whether our one-sided fear gives a one-sided advantage to the Soviets which they systematically exploit is another question. Whether it would diminish rather than increase the risks of war if we succeed in decisively weakening the military and political-psychological strength of the enemy is open to debate, but such action seems plausible. Only the American people can—and must—decide whether we have been wise in being more aggressive in words than in action when it comes to this matter and whether we should support the Soviet slaves with forceful, active support when the fire flames up again in Hungary, in East Germany, or elsewhere behind the Iron Curtain.

18 Formosa: Our Chance in the East

When it comes to the Far East, American interests and tasks differ greatly from those in other areas. If elsewhere in Asia and Africa our problem of defense is closely interwoven with the social and cultural progress of peoples in search of foreign assistance, in the Far East we face mostly the military problem, and we can solve it only by military means. Few of the problems of backward societies groping for reform exist in Asia. Except for a few spots in the former Dutch Indies, the Asian peoples had developed their cultures by the time our ancestors were scratching crude images of animals on cave walls. The Asians were studying the principles of right and wrong according to Confucius when the people of northern Europe were going to sea in huge rowboats, wearing horned helmets, and plundering the slightly more advanced peoples on the coasts of England and France.

If our only problems of foreign policy in the Orient are of a military nature, we could, of course, eliminate them by "disengaging" ourselves from Asia completely. General Marshall recommended this when he proclaimed the Korean War to be the wrong war in the wrong place against the wrong enemies. If he had been right, we might drop our military asbestos show-screen in Asia and turn our whole interest and force toward Europe and Africa. But he was mistaken. Our enemy in Asia might look different from our foe in Europe, but he is the same implacable and therefore "right" enemy and is out for our destruction.

Given this military challenge, we had better concentrate on

our defense rather than try to influence Asia in other fields. The leaders of the Orient are not particularly impressed by our way of life. The poor people in the villages, who squeezed the hearts of our fast-traveling do-gooders, enjoy the saving grace of dignity and self-respect, while they hold in low esteem those material achievements that we Westerners take so seriously. While many Oriental leaders listen politely to our suggestions and look hopefully at our dollars, the mass of the people will make their own changes in their own ways, consistent with the truths which they have developed and which they understand far better than we. As far as "progress" and Western action are concerned, we can leave Asia to its own devices.

But despite the vital military importance of Asia to the United States, we have little impressed the Asians by our military ways. True, they recognize our ability to produce bombs and tanks, good-looking soldiers and PX rations, but what they wonder about is how strong our minds and hearts are in the struggle. The reason is that after all the countless words they have heard from us, they have seen our actions and found them different. To educated Orientals, as well as to the unlearned yet wise Asian peasants, high-sounding statements which are not coupled with action are the mark of philosophers rather than successful government leaders.

What led Asians to their deep distrust of American strength was, first, the Korean experience, where they saw us sacrificing our brave youths and then talking ourselves into confusion and disgraceful defeat. Their second lesson was given in French Indochina when we let our French allies be annihilated by the North Vietnamese Communists while the governments of the West stood passively by debating at Geneva and other conference tables. And the third time we lost our military face in Asia was when we scarcely responded to Red Chinese insults, provocation, and killings, while we wavered just as weakly in our support of our friends on Formosa.

Although—and because—the mind of the Orient is subtle, understanding, and mature, the Asians pay little heed to affirmations of good intent. They ask one simple question: "Who will fight, and if fighting starts, who will win?" Unfortunately, what they saw of the Western powers was mainly compromise, debate, and defeat, while the Red forces appeared to be uncompromising fighters and winners.

"Morality and religion," an Indochinese friend remarked to me, "are essential to life. But we are taught these values by our great religious leaders and also by your missionaries. The job of a government is rather to keep us secure from other governments. If your government cannot do that, our spirit, like lovely flowers in the fields, will be trampled under the brutal feet of Communist oppression."

Our defeats and uncertainties have been publicized and appropriately exaggerated by Communist propaganda throughout Asia. Even if everything it claims is not accepted at face value, it succeeds in highlighting the hard facts of continuous Western ransom payments, acceptance of Communist insults, indecisive fighting, and contributions to the reconstruction of "uncommitted" countries which go over to our enemy, while Red China has successfully fought the West to a standstill in Korea, brought the Communist group to power in Indochina, and isolated Formosa, the last organized force threatening Mao Tse-tung and his Asian army of Communism. Understandably, Asia prefers being "non-committed" rather than committing itself to the apparently losing side, that is, our side.

While doubts about America abound throughout Asia, one finds no illusions about Communism anywhere in Formosa. Highly impressive with its vitality and singleness of purpose, its atmosphere bristles with optimism. From one end of the island to the other, I found unanimous determination to destroy Mao Tse-tung's puppet regime and liberate the Chinese mainland.

Before I arrived there, I had read many an alarmist article warning that the Chinese Nationalists on Formosa were in danger of collapsing from within. These articles reported that Formosa was wracked with "internal rot, decay and subversion," and did the American people want to support a government and a people under such conditions? Once there, I found that 99 per cent of all the derogatory information about Formosa and the Nationalist

Government was completely false. After my talks with peasants in small villages and with many soldiers and after my conferences with Generalissimo and Madame Chiang and with all his cabinet ministers, I found absolutely no sign of rot, decay, or subversion anywhere on the island of Formosa. On the contrary, I found a Chinese nation reborn.

The Chinese Nationalist army thoroughly convinced me of its high military standards. I noticed many small yet significant symptoms of its worth; for example, I didn't see a single fat sergeant all the time I was on maneuvers with Chiang Kai-shek's forces. His fighting men are lean and tough as leather, they move like Indian scouts, and they are fast learning the secret of Western military success: teamwork.

From a vantage point overlooking a broad plain in northern Formosa, I watched some four hundred heavily armed troops move into action against an imaginary Communist invasion force. They were less than a quarter of a mile away and there was only sparse cover, yet at no time could I spot more than three uniforms. They moved swiftly and silently. There was no noise except the crack of their rifles. These troops are masters in the art of camouflage. They cover themselves with strips of cloth, dirt and leaves, and attack at full running speed in canvas sneakers. Different from the American soldier, who is always handicapped by the noise from his banging mess gear, the Chinese soldier's mess kit consists of two wooden chop sticks. The only metal he carries is in his weapon and its ammunition.

Four hundred of the best instructors in the U.S. armed forces are the faculty for one of the most intensive training programs I have ever witnessed. It goes on day and night, seven days a week. To head this training program, the men in the Pentagon chose wisely. They sent to Formosa a pair of able, tough-minded former cavalrymen, Major General William C. Chase and Major General John C. Macdonald. Though both officers are now retired, their systems live on. General Chase, who has great faith in the fighting potential of the Nationalist troops, set up what is called MAAG (U.S. Military Assistance Advisory Group). He is the fighting general who led the spearhead units of the First

Cavalry into Manila and later into Tokyo during World War II. The army section, including the troop-training program, was created by General Macdonald, whom I have admired for years as a former fellow cavalry officer. In my opinion, there is not a better training officer in the world than this much-decorated general. Before commanding the Fourth Cavalry Regiment in France and Germany during World War II, General Macdonald had years of experience in training troops at the famed American cavalry school at Fort Riley, Kansas. I had an opportunity to watch his exacting and effective methods when, for two years during the early part of World War II, I served as his plans and training officer.

With such competent hands as these directing their training, Chiang's troops are, man for man, superior to Mao Tse-tung's Communists, who are being trained by the Russians. Having seen its training program in action, I would estimate conservatively that Chiang's modern army would be more than a match for four or five times as many "old-style" Communist soldiers. We do not have to teach Chiang's soldiers the art of infiltration; they know how to get behind enemy lines. We do not have to give them courage or loyalty or the will to fight; they have these things. What we do have to teach them is the science of modern warfare, the art of wholesale killing through teamwork and co-ordination. Our American instructors are showing the Nationalist soldiers how to advance by rush. They are teaching them to synchronize their platoons, their companies, and their regiments, and they are showing them how to co-ordinate everything, from air to water to land attack. Sometimes the progress is slow, but the Chinese GI and his officers are trying hard and are gradually accepting modern techniques, now that they are sold on their effectiveness.

During my visit to embattled Quemoy, the blockade island in Amoy Harbor only two thousand yards from Red artillery, I heard an interesting story from a Chinese sergeant. He told how the American instructors staged a demonstration to "sell" Chiang's officers on the principle of establishing fortifications right down on the beaches. The Chinese preferred to follow tradition and perch their defensive positions high up in the hills. Boats loaded with dummies were placed in the bay to simulate an attacking Red amphibious force. Then, from established beach positions, synchronized machine-gun fire tore into the targets at water level. The Chinese officers were convinced when they saw the fiery tracer display rip through the twilight to mangle the "invaders." "It was enough to scare you," the sergeant confessed. "I wouldn't want to be out there when I saw that pattern of bullets."

When I was there, about sixty thousand Nationalist troops were defending Quemoy, the keystone of Chiang's chain of off-shore islands, and about twenty thousand were protecting Matsu. But one never hears the word "defense" mentioned by Nationalists. The entire round-the-clock training program is keyed to offense, to the day when Chiang will carry out his promise to return to the mainland. At Kaoshiung naval base in southern Formosa, Nationalist "frogmen" are learning under-water demolition methods, and Nationalist naval assault units are constantly rehearsing amphibious landing operations.

Chiang's entire armed forces now number about 600,000 men, most of them in the army. The Nationalist naval forces count only 40,000 men and have seven destroyers, sixteen minesweep-ers, and a number of landing craft and junks capable of carrying troops. The Nationalist air force is quite weak. It has only a few hundred combat planes, including a sizable number of Thunder-jets and some F-86 Sabrejets, but I was told that the best of Chiang's pilots are rapidly learning the latest combat techniques from their American instructors.

Before going to Formosa, I had heard that Chiang had an army of old men unworthy of American support. I found this to be as untrue as most other derogatory remarks you hear in this country about Chiang, his rule, and his army. The average age of the soldiers in the Nationalist army is twenty-eight. Our own jet fly-ing aces in Korea had an average age of twenty-eight, with all other types of fliers closer to thirty-three. From experience, mili-tary men have decided they don't want an army younger than this. They well remember the unhappy experience of the French, who before the first world war believed that lads in their late teens made the best fighters and therefore concentrated on seventeen- and eighteen-year-olds; we know what happened at Sedan when the French were hit by the more mature Germans. It has been my experience that young men often panic, while older soldiers stand and fight. The twenty-eight-year average for Chiang's army is particularly young, considering that most of his soldiers have never ridden in a truck. They have walked all their lives, working hard and building up their resistance. Physically, a Nationalist soldier is probably the equivalent of an Occidental ten years younger.

The Nationalist military leaders were persuaded to adopt the U.S. military staff system, which is regarded as the world's best, and this action has already eliminated a great deal of waste motion. A Nationalist division is a complete tactical and administrative unit, just as in the American army. Division maneuvers such as I witnessed are employing all of the tactical techniques of modern warfare, from synchronized artillery fire to musketry.

The entire Nationalist army is now becoming adept at grazing fire, such as was introduced to the defenders of Quemoy. Before American instructors arrived, the Chinese were using the obsolete plunging fire. The traditional Oriental method called for getting on high ground to shoot down at the enemy, a hangover from medieval days, when soldiers used swords and those standing on high ground had a great advantage over their climbing attackers. Plunging fire wastes ammunition; a bullet that misses buries itself in the ground. But grazing fire places gunners on ground level and enables them to rake an attacking enemy eight hundred yards. Bullets fired in this manner can kill the enemy anywhere along the invasion path, and they are especially effective in repelling landings.

Along with their military instruction, Chiang's troops receive intensive political indoctrination. This system of political officers, right down to platoon level, seems in our eyes reminiscent of the Soviet commissar system of "political commissars," which was abandoned during Russia's war with Finland. It leads to par-

allel command, which contradicts the single-responsibility philosophy of American commanders. For this reason, U.S. training
officers have been advocating the American system, contending
that split responsibility handicaps the training of troops in purely
military matters.

Yet the Chinese system seems to have its merits in the Nationalist army. As the Nationalist minister of propaganda explained
to me, "Chiang's soldiers come from all parts of China. They
speak many different dialects. To make them successful soldiers,
we must teach them what they are fighting for and that their one
big job is to fight. This can only be done by training a soldier's
mind as we train his body."

As I rode about the trench-scarred fortress island of Quemoy,
I observed some of the work of General Yung, the "political
commissar" of the area. On the western part of this small island,
there are three different statues of Nationalist soldiers. The first
soldier has a rifle slung on his back and a broad smile on his face.
The second soldier, going west, carries his piece at port. The
third soldier is a wooden monument; he carries his weapon at
the ready and stares defiantly at the Red foe on the mainland. To
Westerners, this endless repetition of slogans, expressing the determination to return to the mainland soon, would seem rather
dull. Not so with Orientals, who apparently welcome the assurance that comes from these ever repeated symbols. In all my
travels, I have never seen better morale than among the Chinese
Nationalist troops and the civilian population of Formosa.

Before I went to Formosa, I had heard that Chiang could not
support his army in addition to the normal population of Taiwanese and the "parasites" who had descended on the island
from the Chinese mainland. What I discovered was that Taiwan's
food imports and exports are well balanced. Formosa is rich in
food; for this reason it had been a prize Japanese possession for
fifty years as it sent millions of tons of food, everything from rice
to bananas, to Japan. So far from starvation is Formosa today
that it can export its surplus food products. According to China's
Central News Agency reports, the cane-sugar quota was in-

creased from 727,000 metric tons in 1956–57 to an all time high of 850,000 tons in 1957–58. Of this, 750,000 tons were available for export to other countries.

A great band of fertile land stretches some 245 miles from north to south along Formosa's western half. Most of this rich land, combined with the wet, semitropical climate, produces three crops a year. The ensuing food surplus is more than adequate to feed not only the population of 7,000,000 living there when the Japanese departed at the end of World War II but also the 1,500,000 Chinese (including Nationalist troops) who have arrived from the Chinese mainland since 1949. While Nationalist China is exporting food and adequately feeding its own people at the same time, Red China exported 207,000 metric tons of rice to Ceylon in exchange for 50,000 tons of rubber at a time when, by its own admission, more than 300,000,000 people on the mainland of China were "short" of food and desperately in need of rice.

Another rumor I had often heard and read was that the natives of Formosa, the Taiwanese, hate Chiang Kai-shek. I went to Formosa looking for resentment against Chiang and his troops, but instead of this, I encountered only the belief among Taiwanese that Chiang has done more for them in a decade of government than the Japanese had done in fifty years of occupation. The Japanese improved railroads, built power plants, and spurred industrial development, but Chiang has given the farmers of this agricultural island the ownership of their own land and has improved the general standard of living.

Accompanied by several officers of the Nationalist army, I wandered through various sections of the island and to the outskirts of Tainan, on the southwestern coast of Formosa. Several times my Chinese companions asked directions of Taiwanese, some well dressed and prosperous, others city urchins. The responses were always friendly and co-operative. You can't bluff in things of this sort. If there is resentment, it shows. These people were visibly optimistic and confident about the present and the future. And there is surely no resentment against Americans despite a Communist-inspired riot at the U.S. Embassy in 1957. Americans are popular with Chinese and Taiwanese alike. About midnight one night, I watched two American airmen who had obviously just arrived, probably with some of the new jets being supplied to the Nationalists. "Hey, Chang," yelled one at a man standing in front of a shop, "where can we get some beer?" When I last saw them, they were being escorted by the shopkeeper three blocks down the street to a cafe where they might obtain a fairly good glass of beer at a reasonable price.

Most of the hostile talk about Formosa, of course, is directed against Chiang Kai-shek, the "old, corrupt, greedy war lord." Chiang Kai-shek's name means "unyielding rock," and in all truth, this is what the soft-spoken man in the unadorned uniform appears to be today. As commander of 600,000 fighting men, he promises that the Chinese Nationalist armed forces will fight, to the last man if necessary, to defend Formosa, the nearby Pescadores, and the chain of Nationalist-held blockade islands within shouting distance of the Red Chinese coast. As president of Nationalist China, he is giving the 8,500,000 inhabitants of Formosa an important goal in their fight against the Communist enemy.

Chiang's program on Formosa follows the pattern established by the Western Allies in Berlin during the four and one-half postwar years I was American military governor. We Americans, along with the British and French, bolstered West Berlin's economy and insisted on an honest, democratic government. The contrast to the Communist puppet regime and the deprivation in Soviet-occupied East Berlin was a hands-down victory for the West. In a similar vein, Chiang's Formosa is today a show-window which deeply impresses people behind the Bamboo Curtain.

While the Peiping Reds have made "purge" the most fearsome word in the mainland Chinese vocabulary since more than 50,-000,000 were killed by the Communists, Chiang's new Nationalist government has made the modernization of Formosa pay handsome dividends on both sides of the Formosa Strait. The Nationalists now have solid evidence that the news of their successful Formosa "experiment" is filtering into the most remote mainland villages and hamlets. This is how they are preparing the popular uprising against the Reds, the day that Chiang and his troops will storm back across mainland beaches.

The Generalissimo and his advisers are all agreed that their military victory must be accompanied by immediate and sweeping reforms along the lines tried and tested in the Formosan "model." At the top of the Formosa "showcase" stands Chiang's popular land reform. More than 40 per cent of the former tenant farmers now own their own land. And with this new incentive, more food is being produced, the living standard has gone up throughout the island, and food exports and imports have been balanced. Under the Japanese occupation, many tenant farmers had been forced to deliver more than 55 per cent of their crops to the landlords. Chiang's first step was to reduce this to 37.5 per cent. The tenant farmer is free to.dispose of his share as he chooses. He has a minimum rental agreement of six years, with option for renewal, and his purchase of the land is encouraged.

When Chiang arrived on Formosa in December, 1949, he found more than 20 per cent of all arable land in government hands. He insisted that this be sold to the native farmers at the reasonable price of two and one-half times the annual yield, with payments in commodities rather than in cash stretched over ten years. There was no Communist-style expropriation of holdings. Agricultural and engineering colleges have been established, and modern methods have been introduced in agriculture, industry, and commerce.

Chiang's rule extends from Taipan to the offshore islands, and while we find social and economic progress on Formosa, most of the work on the offshore islands is aimed at military progress. In fact, as I found after six weeks of personal observation in the area, these Nationalist-held offshore islands—Quemoy, Matsu, and others nestling against the Red-held mainland—are the most valuable pieces of real estate in the Far East today and are America's best assets in Asia.

These islands enable Chiang Kai-shek's Nationalists to bottle up Mao Tse-tung's Red regime with an effective blockade along a vulnerable area of strategic coastline. As long as they remain in Nationalist hands, they prevent the Communists from attempting an amphibious invasion of Formosa, and they offer ready-made steppingstones for Chiang's eventual counter-offensive to liberate his Chinese homeland. Chiang Kai-shek is therefore right in his determination to hold these islands, with or without help from the United States, and my inspection left me without a doubt that they can be held. In fact, they must be held or our entire position in Asia will crumble.

After the great blow to our prestige suffered when we talked Chiang into withdrawing from the Tachens and other islands at the northern end of his offshore line in 1955, we could not withdraw for psychological reasons, even if the strategic reasons were not as strong as they actually are. If Quemoy and Matsu and the other islands of this strategic line were ever abandoned, we would confirm Mao Tse-tung's claim that America is nothing more than a "paper dragon." In Asian eyes today, our defense of the Nationalist islands is the final test case.

Most of the names of these islands are unknown to us, and some of them appear as mere dots from the air, at low tide almost within walking distance from the mainland. One cannot understand the importance of Quemoy and Matsu unless one remembers that they are only two links in a long chain of islands which stretches from the mouth of China's most important river, the Yangtze, at Shanghai, all the way down to the British crown colony of Hong Kong.

Since the northern islands were abandoned in 1955 to the Reds, the remaining blockade islands, the biggest of which are Quemoy and Matsu, now hold greater importance than ever. By their control of these islands, the Nationalists still maintain an effective blockade of China's two most important rivers to the south, the Min and the Lung. Opposite the mouth of the Min and the city of Minhow lies Matsu, and the mouth of the Lung at Amoy is faced by Quemoy, which, with its 60,000 Nationalist troops, blocks Amoy's harbor. Mao and his fellow-Communists are most eager to get their hands on these islands because they constitute a serious military threat to the mainland and also because they impose a heavy economic burden on the Reds, whose economic system depends a great deal on river and coastal shipping. Water transportation is the chief bastion of Chinese Communist strength, and when the Reds are deprived of it, their economy will limp along on semistarvation levels.

The Chinese mainland, with almost 4,000,000 square miles of territory and a population of 600,000,000, has only 15,000 miles of railroads altogether; how badly it is equipped can be seen in a comparison with the 226,000 miles of railroads in the United States whose land area is less than that of China. It is the same with other means of land transportation. Red China owns 40,000 trucks, while we count 10,000,000, and Red China has no modern roads to speak of either.

Given this backwardness, which it will take a very long time to overcome, Red China is badly hurt by the fact that it cannot avail itself of the economic advantages connected with the islands under Nationalist China's control. Even Amoy, which has often been called the best "invasion harbor" for a Red strike against Formosa, has no major railroad; its only connection with the interior is an old though recently improved highway. Without coastal shipping lanes for a build-up, the Reds can neither mass troops nor invasion craft at Amoy or anywhere to the north short of Shanghai.

When I flew to Quemoy to inspect its fortifications, the Nationalist commanding general, Liu-yu Chang, told me—and his opinions reflected those of his troops and of the civilian population: "We will fight for these islands and hold them. Even the civil population has taken an oath to stay here and support us. In 1949, which was the last time the Communists came, 17,000 Reds attacked, and 17,000 Reds were annihilated." General Huang Chih, commander-in-chief of the Nationalist army, proved to me that with U.S. support, the Nationalists could "bury the dreams of Mao Tse-tung" on Quemoy if the Reds ever sought to stage a frontal assault.

Since amphibious troops must be highly trained and are much more difficult to develop than ground troops, it seems certain that the 250,000 Red soldiers opposite Quemoy might take the island, as things now stand, but that at least half of this force would go to watery graves. On the other hand, a firm American policy to hold the offshore islands could easily keep Communist troops from ever reaching Quemoy. No troops, however well trained, can cross two thousand yards of rough water on barn doors the way the Russian hordes crossed the narrow Oder River into Germany. The best time to stop an amphibious operation is before it starts. Few places in the world today are better suited for the use of our tactical atomic weapons than is the Red mainland opposite Quemoy. Since it is open country, tactical atomic weapons would devastate the purely military targets of an enemy out for our destruction, while little, if any, danger of injury to the civilian populations would be involved.

In their propaganda, the Chinese Communists, who cannot even conquer the offshore islands, claim that they can—and will—conquer Formosa itself. Until world Communism adopted its present smile-and-murder method, hardly a day passed without a boast from Radio Peiping that the Chinese Communists were on the verge of "liberating" the Nationalist bastion of Formosa. In the fall of 1958, they showed—despite their renewed and rabid claims that they were ready to "liberate" Quemoy and Matsu—that they were unable to do even that. The military truth is that the Reds have about as much chance of seizing Formosa by frontal assault today as they would of capturing Okinawa. Nor is it possible for Generalissimo Chiang Kai-shek to stage a successful invasion of the Red-held mainland under today's conditions. The big military picture in this delicate area right now resembles a stalemate, but in the long run, the situation is far from static.

During my observation tour of the Far East, I made a careful study of the relative military strengths of Mao Tse-tung and Chiang Kai-shek, who have been bitter foes on the battlefield for nearly thirty years. The statistics all seem to favor Mao, but in my judgment, the Red claims of strength are vastly exaggerated. Mao now claims an army of 2,900,000 men backed by a "home guard" of about 1,700,000 and security troops numbering about 1,000,000. His navy, according to Red claims, consists of nearly 400 vessels, most of them small; the biggest craft are several light three thousand–ton cruisers and small submarines supplied by

Russia. Mao's new air force claims to have nearly 3,000 planes, mainly jet fighters. He also is reported to have two or more divisions of Russian-built light jet bombers.

Arrayed against this line-up, Chiang Kai-shek has a combined force of about 600,000 troops on the island of Formosa and the chain of offshore islands fronting the mainland. His navy's largest vessels are destroyers, and he has approximately 500 combat planes.

The edge, on paper, is all Mao's. But it would be a great mistake to assume that on the strength of this seeming superiority, the Reds could take Formosa. For one thing, the Chinese Communist army is poorly equipped and poorly trained, despite the efforts of several hundred Soviet military advisers. By Western standards, Mao's army is still primitive. And what is probably even more decisive is the question of his soldier's reliability. Surely they accept his food, ammunition, and orders and are subjected to intensive indoctrination, but for the most part, they are not Communists. According to the most reliable intelligence sources, there is no indication that the vast majority can be led to accept the Communist philosophy.

The lingering opposition among the Communist troops has been borne out by the continuous and large number of desertions and by the wholesale disavowal of Communism by Chinese prisoners in the Korean War; they forced Peiping to conduct a series of sweeping purges throughout its armed forces. Korea was a test case, not only of Communist morale, but also of military skills, and while overwhelming in numbers, the Reds turned out to be poorly trained and equipped. They have improved since, as the Communists work feverishly to train their troops with Soviet equipment and Russian advisers, but they are still not first-rate troops when it comes to modern warfare. There is a vast difference between armored divisions on paper and their ability to maneuver tanks, fire up-to-date weapons, maintain sensitive equipment, and fight in "Western style." In contrast, more than four hundred American experts are teaching the forces of Chiang Kai-shek to fight in the most advanced Western style, that is, teaching them to save their own lives while destroying the enemy with effective use of modern weapons.

If we continue to send equipment to the Nationalist troops and if they continue their present training progress, it seems to me that the massive forces of Mao Tse-tung would have great difficulty taking Formosa, even without interference from the U.S. Seventh Fleet. The essential bottleneck would be the attempt to cross one hundred miles of open water in Formosa Strait with the invasion craft. If Mao relied on junks, even those with motors, it would take probably twenty hours for the crossing. During this time, the invasion fleet would be at the mercy of Chiang's air and sea forces, to which the recent delivery of U.S. fighter-bombers has given a new punch. For these reasons, there is little risk right now of the Reds trying to assemble an adequate invasion fleet opposite Formosa; there is certainly no such risk while the Nationalists control the offshore islands and thereby deny the Reds the use of coastal shipping lanes from Matsu on the north to Quemoy on the south. As long as the Nationalists maintain observation posts along this chain of islands, they are able to report Red ship movements around the clock. Fighter-bombers from Formosa would report any attempted Red invasion build-up along the China coast opposite Formosa. For a successful invasion, Mao would need air and sea supremacy, and to gain control of the air around Formosa, he would need more jet aircraft and probably direct assistance by Russian pilots.

When the Reds were broadcasting their sharpest threats three years ago, they had few airfields near Amoy; in the meantime they have worked night and day, as in North Korea, to perfect old fields for jet use and to build new ones opposite Formosa. Before, the Communists had only those fields near Quemoy that were built by Major General Claire Chennault when he commanded the famous "Flying Tigers."

Could Mao mount an airborne invasion of Formosa? The answer is yes—if he wants to lose his troops. Any airborne invasion is effective only as part of a large-scale land or amphibious operation. To drop airborne troops on a far-off island, with limited air support and no amphibious follow-up, would be to invite their annihilation, as we learned in the case of crack British and American airborne troops sent against the Germans at Arnheim and Nijmegen during the last war. The inability of Allied ground forces to establish contact resulted in a costly failure of the operation. Moreover, Mao cannot claim first-class airborne troops. The Reds are training paratroopers and glider forces with Russian help, but there are no troops in the Orient today to compare with American and British airborne units. And even the best airborne troops could take Formosa only in co-ordination with a huge amphibious invasion force, of which Mao has none. In addition, tremendous logistical problems would come up with such an overwater operation. Even across the comparatively narrow English Channel, the combined forces of Britain and the United States, backed by the greatest industrial output in the world, were able to land on the coast of France fewer than 1,000,000 soldiers between June 6 and July 2, 1944. During the same period, the Allies had to land 1,500,000 tons of supplies, including 171,000 vehicles and hundreds of tons of other equipment, in order to support their troops ashore. Mao cannot do this.

For all these reasons, even Mao must admit the physical impossibility of taking Formosa against Chiang's fighting footsoldiers and American control of the sea and air. As long as the China problem remains to be fought out between Nationalist and Communist Chinese, the possibility that it will most likely be waged with conventional weapons also remains. What would happen if the Chinese Communists, with Russian approval, attacked Formosa with atomic weapons is another matter. It must be assumed that if the Communists used Russian-supplied atomic shells or bombs, the forces of Chiang could hold their own only if supported by American-furnished atomic power of equal or superior quality. We would certainly be treaty bound to give them such aid.

But if Chiang would use such weapons first in order to destroy the Red invasion force before their departure from the mainland, we can take it for granted that the Soviet Union would supply atomic aid to their Red ally. The local war might well lead to

World War III, whose horrible, half-hidden, ever present threat has caused the Western world to make continuous concessions. Excluding the use of atomic or hydrogen weapons, can Chiang successfully invade the mainland? Given sufficient air and amphibious support by the U.S.A., I believe he can.

The Nationalists, who are maintaining close contact with the mainland, have much evidence to show that their carefully timed liberation move would be widely supported by the masses of Red China. As American-trained General Sun Li-jen told me on Formosa, the powerful, well-trained, and well-disciplined Nationalist invasion force could win the population from Mao Tse-tung and his Communists in short order.

I can well believe this, for dictatorships can crumble overnight, despite their seeming strength. I saw it happen in Guatemala, which I had visited before the successful overthrow of the Communist-dominated government of Jacobo Arbenz. Judging from the lavish display of posters and ubiquitous propaganda outbursts, one would have thought that even the Mayan Indians supported the Guatemalan Communists, yet three hired pilots with three borrowed airplanes finished the business of overthrowing the Communist government of Guatemala. A strong invading force of Nationalists could achieve a similar feat in Red China today.

The lack of popular support for the Peiping Communists has many reasons—the widespread and serious food shortages, the endless series of Red purges, public trials, and executions, the systematic murder of at least fifty million civilians, and the imprisonment of eight million Chinese by the Communists during the operations of the "Labor Reform." Twelve million Chinese slave laborers have been enlisted every year to build waterways and communication projects, while a million others have been sent to Soviet Russia and its satellite countries.

The effects of this permanent blood bath on present-day Chinese moods was pointed out to me by one of the men best qualified to judge the mood of the Chinese people, Marshal Hsi-shan Yen, one of the twenty-nine war lords who called on Chiang to fight Japan after the Japanese attack on China. At the time, Chiang agreed to set aside their petty differences and fight the common foe, the Japanese, as well as the Chinese Communists. As Marshal Yen sees the line-up of forces against the Red government, there are, first, 30 per cent of the people who reject the principles of Communism because they are foreign to Chinese tradition and thinking. Second, many others oppose them because they have come to hate the Communist purges and brutalities. Third, some resent the government's emphasis on industrialization and road-building instead of the consumer goods they desperately need. The fourth and greatest source of opposition stems from personal experiences with the Communist way. Take, for instance, the farmer who must give all of his crops to the Red government, before he is permitted to buy back a small amount, and receives a check for the produce. He has to hand the money over to the government bank, from which he cannot withdraw it unless the local official certifies that it will be used for a stateworthy purpose. As Marshal Yen stressed, only military force can overthrow the Red government, but a good reform program well realized will win the support of the Chinese people. The government of Nationalist China on the beautiful green island of Formosa lives up to this goal. It is our strong ally and our strong hope, together with the Communist-enslaved masses behind the Bamboo Curtain, who are willing, if not waiting, to join us in the fight for freedom.

Mao Tse-tung and his Soviet-backed regime today constitute the greatest immediate aggressive threat to the free world. Our tragic bungling in Korea has inflated the Red Chinese with delusions of power, and they will now do everything they can to expand their areas of control. The time for talk, tough or otherwise, in Asia is past. The time has come when Mao and his troops should know that they will face annihilation if they make one more aggressive move toward the Nationalist-held offshore islands or anywhere else in the Far East. The pledges written and implied in our treaties with the free government of China and SEATO must be unequivocally supported.

And this time we must not repeat the errors of Korea. Any new Red aggression anywhere should be the signal for us and our allies, including the Nationalists of Chiang Kai-shek, to

mount an attack and never let up until Mao and his Peiping conspiracy have been completely destroyed. There can be no moral
question involved in any such attack on Mao Tse-tung with any
weapon or weapons, be they military, political, or psychological,
since Mao and his henchmen have seized illegal control of a
populous nation and rule it in a lawless, murderous way. They
launched an unprovoked attack against us in Korea and have
directly caused the deaths of at least 30,000 Americans and in-
juries to 170,000 more. They have ignored international agreements, insulted us, threatened us, and are preparing to attack us
again. To talk of drawing lines beyond which Mao will not be
permitted to advance is pointless. We have drawn more lines than
a child playing with his blackboard. Mao merely erases them if
and when it pleases him.

The strongest force restraining Mao's Red armies from march-
ing against the British in Hong Kong and on into Southeast Asia
—or from resuming the war in Korea—is the presence of Chiang's
Nationalist troops on China's flank. We can convert this restraining force into a real striking threat. We must step up our training
of the Nationalist troops, arm them with our latest weapons, and
aid them in every possible way. At the least, such a Nationalist
force will be a restraining influence on the militant, aggressive
Red Chinese. At the most, it could be the decisive factor to turn
the tide of war in favor of the forces of democracy in the event
Mao starts a new war to the north or south. There is no better way
to defeat Communism in the Far East than by helping this army
of real Chinese patriots who have dedicated their lives to driving
out Mao Tse-tung and the Moscow puppets who now enslave the
Chinese people.

In the British colony of Hong Kong, though, I heard a different
proposal: "Let us neutralize Formosa, and to make Mao Tse-tung
recognize this neutrality, let him have the offshore islands." Five
hundred miles southwest of Formosa, Hong Kong is today
crowded with Chinese refugees from Communism. But the British
are conducting business pretty much as usual. In British eyes,
Hong Kong means trade. Their crown colony, which consists of
an island and a peninsula, offers a valuable market place around

the finest and most beautiful deep-water harbor in the Far East. They cannot seem to see why politics has to interfere with their business at Hong Kong and have therefore recognized the Peiping Communists as China's legitimate government. At the same time, however, they remain members of SEATO, whose Charter denounces the Reds and their aggressive policies.

The British want to hold Hong Kong, by force if necessary. It can indeed be militarily defended, provided the British are able to muster sufficient planes to control the air while Chiang Kai-shek's Formosan forces keep threatening Mao's flank. When I told the British military commander in Hong Kong, Lieutenant General Cecil Sugden, that I had heard that the Communists could take Hong Kong whenever they chose, he growled: "Anyone who tries to take Hong Kong will get himself a bloody nose."

Whether you laugh at this or agree that the Reds cannot take Hong Kong, you cannot doubt that the British will fight to defend it. The days of the "Colonel Blimps" are gone. I found a young and spirited British army in Hong Kong. The guns don't point the wrong way anymore, as they did at the start of World War II, and most of the British fighting men at Hong Kong are manning strong positions on the peninsula above Kowloon, where they, in fact, should be rather than in barracks and social clubs several miles away from the Red frontier.

It seems a strange contradiction that the British would like to see Chiang Kai-shek and his Nationalists quietly disappear. The reason is that this would simplify their whole far eastern policy and enable them, in good conscience, to carry on full diplomatic and, above all, commercial relations with the Communists in Peiping. The United Nations embargo against the sale of arms and strategic materials to Red China has slowed the traffic, and Britain has therefore insisted upon relaxing the restraining trade regulations. Peiping, on its part, wants to obtain Hong Kong dollars from its sales and deposit them in Hong Kong banks. In return, it can obtain sterling credit in London and use it in Europe, particularly in the eastern European countries, to buy materials for its heavy industries and war preparations.

The British at Hong Kong are making a sincere effort to live up to the UN embargo against the Chinese Communists, but they feel that the China embargo should be less severe, since the embargoes against the Communist satellites in Europe have been relaxed almost to the point of nonexistence. A British official in Hong Kong offered this explanation: "We don't ask a man the color of his skin or the nature of his political beliefs as long as he doesn't break the law or cause trouble. If he minds his own business, we treat him as we have been treating other businessmen here for the past one hundred years." This traditional British colonial tolerance and sympathy with the downtrodden seems admirable, but it is badly misplaced in dealing with present-day Communism and handicaps the defense of the free world. All attempts to "neutralize" the forces of Chiang Kai-shek, on the offshore islands or anywhere else, are unrealistic and shortsighted. We must also reject similar suggestions, even if they come from American "experts," who claimed only yesterday that the Chinese Communists were merely friendly "agrarian reformers" and who succeeded in smearing Chiang in American eyes by means of a gigantic character assassination.

We can no more neutralize the anti-Communist forces of Chiang Kai-shek in the Far East than we can neutralize the anti-Communist forces of the North Atlantic Treaty Organization in Europe. We refused to neutralize West Germany, as the Russians and their fellow-travelers have been—and still keep—suggesting. We prefer to maintain that a powerful western Europe is the best guarantee against an attack by the Soviets. And has any concession to Communism ever brought peace or even a respite from the Communist offensive? Didn't we learn our lesson in 1950 in "neutralizing" Chiang when we shut off our shipments of arms and war materials to his Nationalists while the Soviet Union was rushing war materials to the Chinese Communist armies? We have paid dearly for these mistakes of the past. We must not repeat them. We must throw all of our power behind Chiang Kai-shek and the ultimate goal of a free Asia.

As this book goes to press, the Reds are again shelling Quemoy intermittently. They have been doing it since 1955. The summer of 1958 shelling was the most intense. It stopped after the Reds had fired 600,000 big shells because of three strong reasons: first, they ran out of ammunition; second, they were shot out of the air by superior Nationalist flyers and American-supplied "Sidewinders," those inescapable air-to-air missiles; third, the United States didn't panic into abandoning our responsibilities and allies in the Far East. As long as these three aces remain in our hand, the Reds are not likely to go all out to take Formosa. I say this despite the fact that the Chinese Reds are smarting under their August, 1958 defeat and are anxious to divert attention from internal problems by creating an external danger.

PART FIVE

Looking Forward

19

A Foreign Policy Finds America

Can we conclude our travelogue with one of those "famous last words" which sum up all the world's problems and tell us what to do about them, all in one nice, neat, economy-size capsule? Whenever trouble starts anywhere, one answer, one slogan, one phrase would teach us how to solve it—according to this easy method. I shall not even attempt to present such a conclusion. The challenges of world affairs are too complicated, foreign policies are too complex, and the actions required here and now are too different from those needed there and tomorrow to offer such an easy road. There exists no patent medicine with which we can cure the world's ills, nor is there an all-embracing solution to world problems.

Never in the past has American foreign policy been led according to one clear-cut doctrine. It was always dictated by practical, short-term aims. When it was successful, it was morally purposeful, practical, positive, and dynamic. Today, its long-terms aim is the survival and victory of freedom and faith as we uphold them in this country.

It is for you to judge how well or how badly we have met challenges. Since the end of World War II, we have proclaimed a policy of containment, which did not contain the Soviets, and we have proclaimed a policy of liberation, which did not liberate anyone. We were prepared only and always to "peacefully co-exist" with the Soviets, and for this they were not prepared. In fact, they have been determined to advance into our spheres whenever and wherever they saw a chance to do so without a risk. From our premature demobilization in the postwar years to our failure to use our atomic monopoly to end the Korean war and our failure to support the uprisings behind the Iron Curtain, we have given in to the Soviets. But where we resisted them —economically in Greece and Turkey, politically in Iraq, Berlin; and in Quemoy and Matsu—they were forced to retreat without much counter-resistance.

As we have seen, from Ghana to Berlin and from Cairo to Taipan, the Communist advance continues everywhere, and we must resist it wherever it threatens the far-flung defenses of this country and the free world. As we have also seen, there is no general prescription of a means by which we can do so intelligently and efficiently. But slogans rarely guide us to intelligent and efficient action.

We have discovered that "anti-colonialism" is a slogan which might easily lead us into dangerous traps and that it is equally misleading to talk of a "decaying Europe." Both slogans have met with response from American public opinion because they are deeply imbedded in our own historical character; they appeal to deep emotions inherent in our national character. But we cannot apply them blindly today.

We sympathize with "anti-colonialism" because America was founded under its banner as the world's first colony to proclaim its independence. But then, as Sir Winston Churchill has recently reminded us, we have our own "colonializing" record, which is not better than and only outwardly different from that of the British and French and other European powers. In our own conquest of North America, we undoubtedly treated the Indians as backward natives, but then we established a reign of freedom, tolerance, and economic drive on our continent. If you denounce the "colonialism" of others, remember our own historical "colonialism" and its beneficial results. The "colonial" powers of Europe have done no worse.

We need allies who are strong and whose conditions permit us to count on them. For reasons of strategic geography, the three big European NATO nations, England, France, and Germany, as well as Spain and the North African territories, are of paramount importance as allies of this kind. To them belongs our first duty of allegiance. To neglect our proved friends as we court the so-called uncommitted and backward peoples would be tragic. But we must not alienate the peoples whose sympathy we need. The art of compromise—diplomacy backed up by power —is needed. To neglect and slight the natives of Africa and Asia in their struggle for a better life would be dangerous, and we must avoid it. We must help them where we can; we have indeed begun doing so with what might be called our "Older Brother Policy." Older Brother, armed with moral and military might, holds those economic resources which enable him to give to the deserving while declining to share with the undeserving. Military might, coupled with moral purpose and material generosity, well represents the strength of the United States.

But the simple fact is that the United States cannot solve all the world's problems and should not attempt to do so. We can give aid to others only for their self-help. We cannot bring about the evolution, growth, and final maturity which they themselves must attain. Our government can turn backward peoples into modern nations just about as easily as it can develop a man into an Olympic athlete by doing his exercises for him and feeding him a perfect diet. We can help them, and must help them, only if they are willing to make use of our help. They must pay for it with their own efforts, for real evolution can come only from within. It can never be imported from without.

The second limitation set on our ability to help others is of an economic nature. There is a point beyond which we Americans cannot go in financing foreign economic growth, and we have neared this point. For our government to finance foreign economies is tantamount to taking the required money from us by means of taxation. Today, more than half of the net earnings of the average corporation is taxed away before one cent goes to its owners. When they finally receive their due, a great share must again be handed over to the tax collector, in some cases more than 90 per cent. What is finally left and spent by the owner, frequently a worker or a family with modest savings, is again heavily taxed by the various states and cities. The steel worker who must report for duty early in the morning is taxed 10 per cent of the cost of the alarm clock that wakes him in time to go to work; he is taxed on his coffee, his bread, and the cigarette he smokes before work; he pays taxes on his train fare or car fare. In short, Americans must pay for the "luxuries" of working. If most of the profits are taxed away, the incentive to work and prosper disappears, and with it goes American economic strength.

Our interests appear in a quite different light when it comes to the Soviet-suppressed captive peoples of Europe and Asia. In contrast to the backward, "anti-colonial" peoples, they are indeed held down, exploited, and abused by their masters, who happen to be our deadly enemies, too. Also in contrast to the backward, "anti-colonial" peoples, the captive nations are ready and able to fight on our side. The Communist threat is bound to diminish, if not collapse, if and when the Communist-captive nations rise up, from Hungary and East Germany to the Chinese mainland. To weaken our common enemy, we must strengthen these peoples in their fight for liberation; to increase our strength, we must stand by our secret allies, or we shall lose even our open allies.

We can preserve the peace only if we are so strong or, which is the same thing, if the enemy is comparatively so weak that even the last Kremlin commissar knows for sure that aggression would mean an end to his rule. Yet he must also know that we are willing to use our strength if need be. We have not always shown this in past years, and we still seem uncertain about it. Yet neither the enemy nor our allies nor those uncommitted nations which might come to our side will respect our strength unless they can be sure that we will not hesitate to apply it for all it's worth. This may seem paradoxical (and it was unknown to old-time pacifists), but war can be avoided in the struggle against total-itarian dictators and would-be aggressors only if we do not fear to take the risks of war. Silly cracks to the contrary notwithstand-ing, "brinkmanship" is indeed the safest way of defending free-dom and peace.

Along this general line, questions, as they arise from day to day and from country to country, must be answered by our foreign policy, even if they cannot be solved. There are few, if any, spots anywhere in the world where our actions do not force us to make a choice between two possibilities and a stand between two risks. What are we to do if things between Algeria and France come to a head or if, say, Ghana turns into a dictatorship on its way to technical progress and joins the Communist orbit, if the tension between a Soviet-supported Egypt and Sudan develops into a crisis, if the Communists intensify their fire on the free island of Quemoy, if new uprisings take place in the captive nations of eastern or central Europe? Any of these things may happen any day and countless others in addition. There are no clear-cut answers. Their solution depends on intelligent American public opinion.

Surely it takes a great amount of intelligence for the average citizen to be aware of his responsibilities, to beware of bad counsel, evil propaganda, and disastrous passivity. In times of crisis, Americans have shown that they are well equipped with all these qualities. What is easily forgotten is that we are approaching a crisis if we do not act in the best interests of our country and of the free world.

To find the right path to victory and to support the leaders walking this path, public opinion must first of all develop a resistance against mere words, whether they are vicious words produced and poisoned by the enemy or lofty words beclouding our grasp of the realities. Rather than rely on slogans, we must search for the facts. The record and the program of the Communist conspiracy for world conquest and world rule are facts clear to anybody who wants to know them. To frustrate this goal is our chief aim. To survive, let alone to win, we must be strong and unafraid to use our strength if it weakens the enemy. Our foreign policy can bring us survival and victory only if we are willing to fight and put our trust in God.